GW00374602

IF I SHOULD DIE...
A DEATH ROW CORRESPONDENCE

Edited by Jane Officer

Foreword by Michael Mansfield QC

New Clarion Press

© Jane Officer 1999

The right of Jane Officer to be identified as the author of this work has been asserted in accordance with the Copyright Designs and Patents Act 1988.

First published 1999

New Clarion Press
5 Church Row, Gretton
Cheltenham GL54 5HG
England

New Clarion Press is a workers' co-operative.

All rights reserved. Except for the quotation of short passages for the purpose of criticism and review, no part of this publication may be reproduced, stored in a retrieval system or transmitted, in any form or by any means, electronic, mechanical, photocopying, recording or otherwise, without the prior consent of the publisher.

This book is sold subject to the condition that it shall not, by way of trade or otherwise, be lent, resold, hired out or otherwise circulated without the publisher's prior consent in any form of binding or cover other than that in which it is published and without a similar condition including this condition being imposed on the subsequent purchaser.

A catalogue record for this book is available from the British Library.

ISBN 1 873797 22 2

Typeset in 11/13 Garamond by Jean Wilson Typesetting, Coventry

Printed in Great Britain by The Cromwell Press, Trowbridge

Contents

To all those attorneys, investigators and support staff in the USA who work unceasingly for justice for their Death Row clients, whether they are innocent or guilty

The Soldier

If I should die, think only this of me:
  That there's some corner of a foreign field
That is for ever England. There shall be
  In that rich earth a richer dust concealed;
A dust whom England bore, shaped, made aware,
  Gave, once, her flowers to love, her ways to roam,
A body of England's, breathing English air,
  Washed by the rivers, blest by suns of home.

And think, this heart, all evil shed away,
  A pulse in the eternal mind, no less
    Gives somewhere back the thoughts by England given;
Her sights and sounds; dreams happy as her day;
  And laughter, learnt of friends; and gentleness,
    In hearts at peace, under an English heaven.

Rupert Brooke, 1914

Foreword

Talk of human rights is presently at a high point in the wake of the anniversary celebrations in 1998 for the United Nations Universal Declaration, and the passing of the Human Rights Act in the UK incorporating the European Convention. For many, however, only the efforts of ordinary people have alerted the conscience of a nation to inequality and injustice. In the UK, the parents of the murdered black teenager Stephen Lawrence are heirs to a tradition of principled protest led in the USA by Martin Luther King. It is often the black community who bear the scars and who then become the torch-bearers.

So it is on Death Row. Among the inmates there are a disproportionate number of black defendants without resources, commonly without adequate representation, and without justice. Some American states are even considering the ultimate degradation of allowing the condemned man's death throes to become a televised public spectacle.

The Andrew Lee Jones Fund has pioneered support for a handful of beleaguered lawyers who are fighting tremendous odds in unspeakable circumstances. Recently another organization in the UK, *amicus*, has sought to complement this support by training and sending volunteer lawyers to help in capital cases.

These letters and diaries from Andrew Lee Jones are as powerful a testament to the human spirit as the diary of Anne Frank or the dramatised work of Sister Helen Prejean in the film *Dead Man Walking*. The book reinforces the urgent need for action in a country supposedly at the heart of western democratic values.

'A man without hope / Is a man without a dream.
And without a dream / A man has no purpose.'
Andrew Lee Jones

Michael Mansfield QC
London, March 1999

Acknowledgements

My most grateful thanks must go to Kerry Collett and Sally Jervis, who volunteered to take on the laborious task of transcribing all Andrew's letters and diaries to disk form.

Thanks to Sarah Ottinger for coming in at short notice and contributing the afterword from the attorney's viewpoint on the case.

Thanks to Nick Trenticosta, Director of the Loyola Death Penalty Resource Center in New Orleans, Andrew's lead attorney at the end, for his involvement with the book.

Thanks also to the ALJ committee for all their hard work and dedication over the past six years, and especially to Sophie Garner, co-founder and secretary.

And finally, but by no means least, thanks to Chris and Tracey Bessant at New Clarion Press for their encouragement and commitment in getting it all together.

Jane Officer

Introduction

Angola, Louisiana's State Penitentiary, lies at the end of a pretty, winding country road edged by old trees hung with grey green Spanish moss and twenty miles from Highway 61. In 1991 the last few miles of the road to the prison were on a dirt track and full of holes. It has since been tarred. Approaching the end of the road to the prison, the radio mast towers above the trees and a bend in the road opens out to reveal the entrance to the 18,000 acre farm which houses 5,000 of Louisiana's high-security inmates in camps spread throughout the prison area. Originally three slave plantations worked by Africans, principally from Angola, it is now a modern-day slave camp with lines of heavily guarded men working in the fields from 'sun up to sun down' for two cents an hour. As Angola is surrounded on three sides by the fast-flowing Mississippi river and on the other by the rattlesnake-infested Tunica Hills, escapes have been few and rarely successful.

To the right of the prison main entrance is a modern brick building with dark, meshed windows. In front of the building is a bright, well-kept garden and a small pond for a resident duck family. The building and garden are surrounded by heavy razor wire and overlooked by a guarded watchtower. This building houses Louisiana's Death Row. In 1991 34 men were incarcerated on three tiers, each in a six foot by nine foot cell and allowed out, alone, for one hour a day to exercise, make phone calls and talk to other inmates down the row. It is a place where men are 'warehoused' for years as their appeals are gradually exhausted and sentences finally carried out or, if they are lucky, commuted to life without parole.

17 July 1991 was exceptionally hot in Louisiana. The temperature exceeded 100 degrees with matching humdity and it was impossible to be out of doors for more than a few minutes at a time. I checked in at the reception hut by the main prison gate at about 10.30 a.m. the

morning after my arrival from England. Even the short walk through the double security gates and across the garden from reception was exhausting for someone accustomed to an English summer. After waiting an hour in the entrance hall of Death Row for a legal visit to be completed, I was finally escorted through the series of iron barred doors to meet, for the first time, my Death Row penfriend, Andrew Lee Jones. As we went through the gates, a guard would call 'Woman on the hall' to warn all the prisoners who worked in this building to keep off the corridors. Through another locked door and up a flight of stone stairs, I was escorted to the visiting area: a small room with four booths whose dark windows were covered in thick wire mesh. I was here to keep a long-made promise to 'set down' and talk with Andrew, and here we were, meeting just five days before he was due to die in the electric chair. I had difficulty seeing his face as he was locked and handcuffed in a tiny cubicle with no light. The mesh on the window was thick and he was black. He could see me quite well as my skin was white and the room I was in had white painted walls and a light was on. There was a fan to cool the room I was in, while Andrew had to sit in the heat, which he was well used to. There is no air conditioning in prison for inmates. We spent a couple of hours together, hardly mentioning his case, at his request, as he wanted to enjoy his time. He asked me many questions about my family, friends and cats, the garden and anything that would banish thoughts of death for a while. James Minton, a reporter from the *Baton Rouge Morning Advocate*, arrived and wanted a picture of us together, but the mesh and the light made this impossible. He went to talk to the major in charge of the guard and arranged for Andrew and me to spend a few minutes in the office next door, so that he could take photographs to illustrate his article, 'The English schoolteacher who has come to visit murderer "Flash" Jones'. Andrew was brought out, handcuffed and shackled, and I was warned not to touch him as it would terminate the visit immediately. Andrew smiled broadly but nervously and seemed to be taking a million little photographs of my face, clothes and jewellery to build up a picture of this friend who had crossed the Atlantic, for the first time in her life, to visit him. I instinctively touched his arm with my hand as he was led away at the end of the visit.

I can clearly remember the last time capital punishment was used in the UK. It was in August 1964, the day before my thirtieth birthday and when my children were aged one and nearly three. Later I remember feeling relieved to know that they would grow up in a country that did not use the ultimate penalty for murder. Capital punishment was not a part of my life in the following years. My children were growing up, I trained as a teacher after nursing for twelve years, my husband died and soon my children left home to lead their own lives. In the late 1970s I joined CND and actively campaigned for nuclear disarmament, taking part in the London marches and, later, several antinuclear demonstrations at Greenham Common. I joined Greenpeace and did local campaigning and collecting for them. These were important human rights issues of the time and I feel proud that I took part in them.

In 1988 I watched, along with many thousands of others, Paul Hamann's BBC documentary *Fourteen Days in May*, chronicling the final days of Edward Earl Johnson prior to his execution in the gas chamber at Mississippi's State Penitentiary. It was moving, shocking, disturbing and, ultimately, haunting. Had I been asked, at that time, how many people I thought were presently imprisoned on Death Row in the USA, how long, on average, they awaited their fate and how good the capital defence system was, my answers would have been wide of the realities which I began to discover.

In May 1990 an article appeared in the *Observer* newspaper. A group of Quakers in Cambridge, England, had responded to the documentary and one of them, Jan Arriens, had written to Sam Johnson, who was imprisoned in the cell next to Edward Earl and who had also appeared in the film. The result had been the opening of a window across the Atlantic and the start of a penfriend organization, called LifeLines, not only for Mississippi Death Row inmates but for the 2,800-plus men, women and juveniles on Death Row throughout the USA at that time. The article described some of the conditions, physical, psychological, medical and emotional, which are daily life on Death Row, and appealed for new writers to meet the demand from prisoners for UK penfriends. The main feeling which struck me on reading the article was the loneliness of being incarcerated for at least five or six years, and maybe up to twenty years, before sentence was passed, commuted or voided. This time was often spent with little emotional support if the prisoner had been abandoned by family, as many Death Row inmates are for the shame, pain and stigma they bring to their families. The life histories of most of the men are sad and violent. Abused childhoods, violence, drugs, prejudice and racism are commonplace, and I was also able to identify with them from my twelve years working with difficult and disturbed youngsters in inner-city schools. How many of those I had known and worked with over the years *could* have ended up in a similar situation? I had seen racism and prejudice at work and witnessed the effects of drugs. I had visited prisons and Borstal, and spent hours in police stations ensuring 'fair play' especially for young black youths. The stories I was reading had strong resonances. And here, also, was my opportunity to respond to *Fourteen Days in May*. I wrote to LifeLines and, within a few days, received the name of Andrew Lee Jones on Death Row in Angola, Louisiana's State Penitentiary.

I did not write immediately. I needed time to consider my reasons and whether they were the right ones to embark on this unknown journey. It was fine in the abstract, but when I had the name of a real person, careful thought was needed. This was to be a commitment which could end with an execution or, with luck, a sentence of life without parole and writing until *I* was dead! I wrote a short, introductory letter and carried it around for a few days, but finally posted it. An answer came through in about ten days – an immediate turnaround. The correspondence began and lasted the fifteen months until and just beyond Andrew's death.

Over the months, Andrew began to unfold his life story to me and to share his thoughts, regrets, fears and hopes. Andrew was quite open with me about the crime for which he was convicted: the killing of his ex-girlfriend's daughter. I learnt fast about legal issues, about life on Death Row and, especially, about loneliness and isolation when it contrasted so much with my own full and happy life. Andrew became part of my life as an 'elder son' – he loved to hear about all the things I was doing day to day, and to share the time with me in writing. He was fascinated to be writing to someone in England and to have a whole new interest in those last months. We wrote at least once a week, and at stressful times I was sending a brief letter or card most days, just to let him know I was thinking of him. He trusted and felt safe with me because I came from outside the USA. None of my letters has survived; they were destroyed in the prison prior to Andrew's execution. But I have more than seventy letters and four diaries that he sent me, from which the extracts in this book are taken. The letters run from June 1990 and the diaries from January 1991. I sent him books and he particularly enjoyed the illustrated books of Wales, which gave him a totally new landscape in which to place himself at times of stress and sadness.

In January 1991, when an execution date had been set, he wrote about his dread of being buried inside the prison. The idea of his body remaining imprisoned after his death was a great fear. It was at that point that I wrote out for him Rupert Brooke's poem, 'The Soldier', to suggest that, wherever he was buried, that place would always belong to him and not the prison. Andrew understood the meaning but was not comforted by the thought. As he wrote to me, 'I wish you hadn't said that the guy's body never made it home. That put fear in my heart. I hate the thought of being left here. After reading the poem, I felt what he felt; he wanted his home land, he wanted to be home. No one should be left in prison or a strange land.' I later learnt that being buried in prison is a dread of all the prisoners, for ever trapped in an unnamed grave with no access for friends and relatives, as if you had never existed.

I was not Andrew's only penfriend. Besides another UK penfriend, he had two or three longstanding US penfriends through the churches and a spiritual advisor who wrote to him and could visit him regularly. He also wrote to and was visited by a young black woman from Shreveport. They had grown to love one another and many of Andrew's letters to me included his concerns when she did not get in touch for a while or her circumstances changed. Later I learnt many of the reasons why his family had not visited regularly despite the fact that they lived only about twenty miles away on the other side of the Mississippi. The family is poor and isolated and has no access to public transport. Andrew's mother, Hazel, could not get to visit without help. Her health is not good and she found the pain of visiting a son on Death Row, and being unable to touch him through the heavy, metal visiting screen, a very hurtful experience. This, I later learnt, is common; for mothers it is a particularly stressful situation. But Andrew was dearly loved by his family and they were with him to the end.

19 July 1991 was the day the Pardon Board met to decide whether to recommend a change in Andrew's death sentence. The only possible alternative was life imprisonment without parole – in effect, another death sentence. Arriving at the prison by 8 a.m., the busloads of family, friends, supporters, lawyers, experts, press and TV cameras were taken the five miles inside the prison to Camp F, which houses the death chamber as well as the teaching rooms used for the Pardon Board meetings. The room was full and the proceedings lasted until almost 6 p.m. Members of the family spoke for Andrew, and I, very nervously, also spoke for him and heard information related to the crime and Andrew's life which was new to me. The prosecution had only one witness, the dead girl's stepgrandfather, who stood up to demand Andrew's death with no mercy. I was shocked by the level of open racism expressed in that room. Andrew was referred to as 'that nigger' by the prosecuting District Attorney.

Hope rested on the issue of the electric chair and whether, in its current state, its use was constitutional. Did it cause 'cruel and unusual punishment'? Several recent investigations had shown how badly the bodies were burnt by the poor state of the equipment, which had been in use for decades, and had demonstrated that death did not occur instantaneously as the prosecution argued. Louisiana had decided to change over to lethal injection from September 1991 and a delay in Andrew's execution would always bring hope. Andrew knew all the details of this debate as he waited on Death Row. The Pardon Board left the room to deliberate and came back to vote for death by lethal injection. A feeling of relief was soon squashed when it was explained that the Governor was sure to press for the electric chair to be used as arranged. Elections were soon to take place and he needed to be seen as tough on crime. Andrew's lawyers made appeals to the state, the Governor and the Supreme Court in Washington right up to the end. They worked non stop, day and night, for that last week of Andrew's life.

At one o'clock on Sunday, 21 July I had a phone call from Neal Walker, one of Andrew's lawyers, asking me to hurry down to the prison. Andrew had asked for me to be there with him and his family for the last visit before his execution. Driving down that road as fast as I safely could, parking the car, clearing security and then being driven across the fields to the death chamber at Camp F was an almost surreal experience. The guard driving the bus played country music and asked curiously why I should want to travel across the world to visit with this 'nigger trash'. He could not understand why we did not have the death penalty in Britain. How else do you solve the problem? Arriving at the visiting room, I could see a long table laid out with a white cloth and around it Andrew's family and his special friend from Shreveport. I joined them and was able to hug Andrew for the first time. Although he was still shackled, at least his handcuffs were removed for these last hours with his family. Soon the men of the family left and until the end of the visit, just before 6 p.m., Andrew's mother, sisters, friend and myself watched time pass, and shared laughter, tears and prayers. Sisters talked of the fun they had had as children, Hazel led frequent prayers during which we all held hands around Andrew. And we waited and watched and hoped for the best from the Governor and then the Supreme Court in Washington. Andrew told me that his ex-girlfriend, the mother of the murdered girl, had phoned him during the day, saying that she was a lawyer and apologizing for what was happening to Andrew. She told him that 'she had never meant for this to happen'.

At one point Hazel asked me to join her in the females' toilet, where she asked me if I would be prepared to take photographs of Andrew's burnt body after the execution to record what the chair did to her son. I agreed, but never had the opportunity.

At a quarter to six the Warden came in and asked us to leave. I hugged Andrew and told him how much I had enjoyed our friendship and promised never to forget him or allow his name to be forgotten. He asked me to take care and also to stop the family from crying in that room so that he could remember happy faces and stay strong himself. His mother was asked, as a last transaction between mother and son, to sign to receive his body after death, and he signed his body over to her. At least he knew now that he would not be in prison for an eternity. We all left, cheerfully, and collapsed together in tears once the doors were closed.

I spent the evening with the family. The house was full of friends and family. Andrew rang all through the final hours. When the Supreme Court turned him down at about 11.15 p.m., his mother started to wail. I recall sitting on a settee with two of Andrew's younger brothers, very drunk and crying, their heads in my lap. At 12.30 a.m. we knew it was all over. In the morning, Hazel rang to collect Andrew's body. It was released to the funeral home, but for the next few hours we were given different reasons why we could not go and view it. We were told that it smelt, that it did not look pleasant and, then, that they were already 'working on it'. I left for my onward journey by way of the funeral home and managed to buy some flowers for Andrew, but I was not allowed to see him for a last goodbye.

At the end, Andrew was tired, with a tiredness that only Death Row inmates know. The years of loneliness, isolation, appeals and imprisonment awaiting a sentence take their toll. As Andrew said so often, those who had not lost their minds before often did so in those years. The longing for everyday things – walking on grass, holding a hand, seeing flowers, eating with friends, having a little quietness – become unreachable but precious memories. He told me that he had reached the end and did not want it all to continue, for the sake of his family and friends and for himself. The thought of life without parole was no more appealing than death.

On the morning following Andrew's execution, the metal workers in the prison workshop were shown plans for building a 'restraint table'. These were immediately recognized as the exact plans for a lethal injection gurney intended to replace the electric chair. The men refused to build it and were locked up. Over the next few days there was a full-scale prison riot which was brought under control only when it was agreed that the gurney would be made by an anonymous Baton Rouge contractor at a cost of $5,000. On 12 September 1991, the heavy oak execution chair, which had been in use since 1941 and in which 77 people had died, was unbolted from the floor of the Death House and removed to the Louisiana State Museum in New Orleans.

Murder is the ultimate crime and I believe that murderers should be punished, but punished justly. Execution has become an act of revenge, not punishment, in the USA. Almost without exception, Death Row inmates are poor and inadequate. Young black men make up the highest numbers overall in proportion to their numbers in the general population. The legacy of slavery remains among the 'killing states' of the south, and, for a liberal, white Briton with close friends of all races and ethnic groups, the racism was a shock. I still do not know, any more than Andrew knew himself, if he did kill that little girl. He always said that he had no clear recollection of that night due to being drunk. He may well have been on drugs too. What is without doubt is that his trial was typical of hundreds of others which take place in the southern states, in that he was represented by a court-appointed lawyer with no capital trial experience and no funding for an adequate defence, and who met Andrew only a few weeks prior to his trial. This lawyer testified *for* Andrew at the Pardon Board hearing and explained his lack of experience and knowledge at the time of the trial in 1984. He was not aware, for example, that Andrew was heavily drugged throughout the trial, which gave the impression that he did not care. Evidence which may have led to a different outcome was never explored or submitted, and there are more questions remaining in my mind than have ever been answered. However, my friendship with Andrew would not have been affected, whatever the true facts of the case. Whatever happened occurred years before we met, and by that time he was a different person; he had 'hit the concrete' of Death Row and taken the years to review his life and to start to rehabilitate himself, as his letters show. He was never given the chance to try and complete that process. I gave my friendship unconditionally.

The experiences of that summer led me to consider setting up a memorial for Andrew based on the promise that I would not allow his name to be forgotten. Standing outside the prison with Andrew's lawyers, after the Pardon Board meeting, all of us feeling tired, shocked, angry and tearful, I asked the question, 'What can *we* do?' The reply was: 'We need more well-qualified, hardworking and dedicated capital defence attorneys.' And so, a few months later, the Andrew Lee Jones Fund was founded to raise money and awareness in the UK and the USA so that students could qualify in capital law in the USA or spend some time working alongside established lawyers to gain experience. To date, two students have completed their studies and are practising in South Carolina and Florida respectively. Sixteen students have spent time as interns assisting lawyers with defence work. One student is presently studying law in New Orleans and intends practising in capital defence.

Since 1991, my experience of Death Row has grown. I correspond with and have visited penfriends on Death Row in Florida and Texas. The friend in Florida has been on Death Row for 24 years. I also write to three men in Angola: one on Death Row; one, now off Death Row, who was a friend of Andrew's on the row; and a man who is serving a life sentence without parole. I visit whenever I can and have come to know their families. In New Orleans I have good friends and, through them, understand more acutely how the death penalty affects and damages so many lives. The families of Death Row inmates are, without doubt, the unacknowledged victims of the system, having to deal with the pain of their loved ones being on Death Row and, in many cases, being executed after many years.

I have no regrets about writing that first letter in 1990, as my life has been all the better for the experiences that have followed, and which continue. While I was in Angola this May, visiting Feltus, who had just received a stay of execution at 36 hours, he asked me and his other penfriend why we are prepared to put ourselves through so much pain. Our reply was that we had promised to be there when he asked us both, seven years previously, and a promise is a promise and cannot be broken.

Jane Officer
Birmingham, England
October 1998

June 1990

4 June 1990

Hi Jane,

How are you and your family at this time? Hopefully, everything is as well as can be. For myself, I'm fine. Anyway, I received your letter today and it surprised me. I never expected to receive a letter from England. Thank you for taking the time to correspond with me. I've been looking for someone to start a corresponding relationship with. I would like very much to get to know you better and what it's like in your part of the world.

Let me start by telling you a lil about myself. I'm 6 ft, 34 years of age, born 24 August 1955. I been here on Death Row since 15 November 1984. I have had seven execution dates. My last one was 28 August 1989. I don't have any children and I don't have any friends here on Death Row. It don't pay to have one because it's no telling when he might get executed.

Execution is part of life here in Louisiana; the Governor, that's what he stands for. Anyway, I'm a man that stays to myself. I like to watch sports and I do a lot of exercise. I keep myself in good condition. If I ever let myself go, it would be the end. We are locked down for twenty-three hours a day. We get to go outside three days a week for one hour. Also, the other four days, we get one hour on the hall. Every time I'm out of my cell I'm handcuffed except when I have the hour on the hall. I'm in a one-man cell. At no time am I on the hall with any one else. Even on the yard, I'm separated from the rest.

The rules here is very hard. The cell that I'm in is right in front of the light and it stay on twenty-four hours. Since I been here, I have seen men lose their minds. I lost count on how many got executed. The guy in the next cell from me talks to his self and he answers his self. It's hard to hold on here but I'll make it. When you write back, feel free to ask any questions. I want to start corresponding with you. Send me a picture. I'll send you one when our time come around again; we only take pictures every three months. Also, you must have my address the same way it's on my letter, okay? So, you take it easy and I'll wait to hear from you.

Peace
Andrew Lee

18 June 1990

Hi Jane,

Your letter arrived today, Monday, and I was glad to hear from you and to know that all is well for you and your family. You take a nice picture also. I will send you one the first chance I get, okay? Also, I am glad that we can start a corresponding relationship but we have one small problem, I can't understand all of your writing. Your writing, in your part of the world, is a lot different from mine and I never took shorthand. Don't get me wrong now, I can read just about all of it, it's just some of the words you have connected together, but I know in time, I will get your writing together.

Anyway, to answer your question of how I got here: In 1984, I broke out of East Baton Rouge Jail, and it took me two weeks to get out of that city. During that time, my girlfriend found out where I was and she brought the police with her – she was driving my car and they were following her. I got away but I still got stuck with her. I lost my car to the police cause they were waiting for me to come get it. Me and my girlfriend, we left Louisiana, and went to Texas. From there, we were going to California, but my girlfriend decided that she didn't want to be on the run any more, but she didn't tell me, she told the police.

It was on a Thursday, the police walked down on me watching TV. I had changed my name to Jesse Lee – I had an ID card and everything. She told them that too. When I was brought back to Baton Rouge, three months afterwards, I was on the go again. During this time, they said that I killed my girlfriend's daughter for her putting the police on me and that's how I got here.

I have been coming close to getting executed. I don't let it get next to me. It's like this, everybody wants to die but no one *really* wants to die. If it came to my time, I'm ready for it and I don't feel bad for being here, for something I didn't do. I look at it this way, I'm here for something I did in the past.

I left home when I was seventeen and no one in my family knew if I was dead or alive. I used to call sometimes and ask if everyone was well. I left home because my father had died and I didn't see any point in staying there any more. I can't say where I went wrong in life but after my father died, nothing else mattered. All I wanted to do was have a good time and dress good. Since I been here, I have had a lot of time to think things over. I think about how I should have been a better person. I didn't have to do all the things I have done. I hate to think how I had turn my back on my family. I was a fool but it's too late now – there's nothing I can do that can change the past.

Anyway, since I been here I have kept a diary – everything that I can remember as a child. When I got your letter, I wrote it in my diary. Matter of fact, I was thinking about sending it to a publishing company but I can't get all the fellows to agree to let me use their names because it also has stuff that went on while I've been here. Who got into it with who, all the executions, the ups and downs I been through, the nightmares I have had. I even make copies of the letters I write. I forgot to tell you that I would like to put your letters in there, if that's okay? I have the space ready right now, it just says, 'Letter from Jane Officer'. If it's okay, I'll glue it in. I also keep time and dates also.

I will write more as time goes by. We will know all there is to know about each other.

Oh, my family call me 'Flash' and I like football, basketball. Really, I like all kinds of sports.

Okay, I've got to go now. I'll wait to hear from you. Also, I'll be going over your letter so that I can understand your handwriting better.

Peace
Andrew Lee

July 1990

Hi Jane,

It was nice to hear from you again, and to know that all is well. How are you and your love ones at this time? For myself, I'll just say, so so. Anyway, I read your letter without any problem – it was just some of your words I couldn't make out.

You talk about that lil Indian guy. It's a guy here that got lock up at fifteen, and he have lost his mind – he is walking up and down his cell talking to his self. A man must have a strong mind to survive here, on Death Row – it's no telling when things is going to turn for the worse. Life here is up and down, a man can't even get a pardon. Either way here is death. Right now, they are trying to bring in lethal injection and outlaw the electric chair, that suppose to stop people from saying how cold it is to put someone in the chair. It's all the same, murder is murder. It's no such thing but legal murder.

Anyway, yes, I'm keeping a diary – nothing to do but think back over my past. One day, I just started writing, and now I'm considering trying to get it publish. Like, I have wrote to some places, and some even ask me to send it, but my lawyer, he said he don't think it's a good idea now because I'm still on Death Row, and when I get a date, everybody that read it is going to know about my past life – and life wasn't good to me.

I must say this: I'm going against my code telling you somethings about myself, mostly because you are not from here. I have had people to trick me, telling me that they wasn't for the death penalty, and they were. When an execution date is set, the news people be showing people with signs that's for the death penalty, and I saw them. I felt like a fool, to think back that I had told them how I was suffering here. I shared my thoughts, my feeling with them, but that was okay. I kept myself strong. I should have known something was funny. One lady I was writing, I ask her to send me a Bible, she send a book about meditations. One lady I told I need a radio. She send a tape player, and it don't serve me no purpose – I don't even have one tape. A lot of people be writing but I don't write back, I guess, I wrote back to you because you are not from here.

It's something to think back on, being here for a killing that I have been sentence to die for, and the hurting part about it, was that at my trial, it didn't have nobody to testify against me. The mother of the girl, she came and visit me every visiting day, and never once ask me whether or not I killed her daughter. I just stop getting in touch with her last year because I found out that she was on the stuff and lost all respect for herself.

I got found guilty for three reason: I was the boyfriend, she had turn me into the police one time, and my lawyer, he didn't have any experiences in handling a death penalty case – he didn't even have five years in (that's how long a lawyer suppose to have in before he can take a death penalty case) and I didn't know that at the time. Two years ago, I got two new lawyers just in time because my time had run out – I had two execution dates in one month and another one a few months after that. They definitely step in at the right time.

Anyway, about my father, yes, we were very close. I don't think that I would have been here if he would have lived. He was a man that didn't do no wrong, he didn't believe in beating a child. After he passed on, I just left home, I just move around a lot. I'm a person that can fit in easy – everyone say it's my eyes that attract people attention.

We don't have a library here. The only way we can get books, if some friend or family member send them. I like to read the book I can get but I like cowboys. I like to read how they were drifting, it remind me of myself. A radio and a book

– that's what mostly pass the time away. Cause, like starting at 5.45 a.m., it's breakfast. I go back to sleep until 10.30 a.m. – that is if they don't have yard call. Yard is just for one hour – Monday/Tuesday/Wednesday. The other four days, we are inside. Anyway, at 11.00 a.m. I watch the news, also. At 12.00, from then to 3.30, it's nothing to do; read a book, lay down. I have watch so much TV, I don't even look at it until the news is on.

If I had another chance of life, I know it would be better. I have had my share of this prison life, being lock up without seeing any family member – it's like no tomorrow. Jane, I'm use to not seeing my family but I look at some of these people here, who were use to seeing their family, I can see the hurt in their eyes, especially when they don't have any cigarette or coffee and don't have the money to get any with – that too can drive a man crazy. Jane, without these things: cigarettes, coffee, radio, visit, yard, TV, letters, books, money, a man don't stand a chance here. I got two of these in my favour – I don't smoke and I don't drink coffee. Three main killers here, is cigarettes, money, visit. I have seen what they did to people who get it.

My neighbour, he don't ever stop talking to his self. The other one, he went to the hold.[*] Like, for coming out on tier for the hour, that might be at 2.00 a.m., the only real peace of mind I get is when I'm watching sports, or on the yard. I just can't stand to look at these same faces everyday. That's why I go on the yard every time they call yard.

Okay Jane, like I'll answer some more of your question next time. I'm not use to writing yet. I had a typewriter but it broke down on me. So, you take it easy and I'll await to hear from you.

Peace
Andrew Lee

The punishment block at Camp J. Andrew is sent there in January 1991. It is also referred to as 'the Hole' because 'It's just what it is – a Hole'.

20 July 1990

Hi Jane,

How are you at this time? Hopefully, everything is as well as can be. Like, the reason why I didn't answer your letter when I first received it, was because I thought may be that I was going to get my pictures in – I wanted to send you one. I don't know why it's taken so long.

Everything here is so so. One guy just gotten turn down – he will be getting a date soon. They are trying to bring in death by injection. I don't know for sure, right now but I do think that the bill have pass. Death is death, no matter how it's carry out – this state just believe in the death penalty.

I tell you Jane, this prison is something else – it's never a day without a change. Like, in the winter time, when we have yard call, we have to go outside with nothing but a jump-suit, under-shorts and a T-shirt, because the coats, they have 30 or 40 other people use them, also. We use to go outside with our own clothes on, but two guys from another camp, jump the fence and so they took it out on Death Row.

Our situation is the worse here. If I happen to go to the hold, I won't get any mail or phone calls until I get out, and that could drive a man crazy. I'm definitely glad that I am strong in many ways. I never let tomorrow's problem get in the way of today's problem. I have learn to take the situation as it come. I have pass through my biggest test – not seeing any family member. I wonder about them and that's about it. Like, the only real problem I have is that if I do die here, would they come and get my body? I don't want to be laid to rest in a prison grave-yard. That would mean that in the after world, I'll still be a prisoner. I do hate that thought.

Anyway, like, my old girlfriend, she didn't really give up on me, I gave up on her. After I came here, I didn't want to see her at that time – I didn't care what tomorrow would bring. I was being put on Death Row for being the boyfriend. I was lost with no hope – life just wasn't life to me then. But after a while, I started thinking about the years that have passed me by, death should have been coming my way.

Anyway, you ask about my lawyers. Yes, they are better than the ones I had at first – the last lawyers I had, I came within 20 hours of death, and they didn't even get it so that I can go before the Pardon Board. They was getting ready to send me over to the Death House – the only thing that save me was that they file and let the courts know that they needed more time, and I guess they knew it too, so they had given them thirty days. During that time, my lawyer Nick, he got in touch with me and wanted to know if he could talk over my case along with another lawyer, name Rebecca, and I said, yes. That was in 1988. Since then, I have had three dates.

I didn't think too much about it when I received your letter, because like I had said, some people write so they can tell their friends how glad they are that I'm suffering. Some write because they care. It's all kind of reason why people write to Death Row inmates. I have a list of people that have wrote to me. The worst one of all was a lady name Judith, from Springdale, Arkansas – that was the name and address on the letter. She wrote, 'May your Christmas be weary, and the electric pass through you dearly.' It was more, but I won't write that down. Anyway, the last guy that got executed here, he got a letter from someone that was so cold, I felt for him. Jane, there are some people in this world that don't have no soul. Sometime, I have to think about opening a letter.*

Once a year, people from churches come to visit us sometime during Christmas. I have a Bible and I do Bible lesson too. I don't know a lot about the Bible by heart, but I have read it a lot.

Okay, you take it easy and say 'hello' and I'll wait to hear from you.

Peace
Andrew Lee

*Andrew later told me that he carried my first letter around for several hours before opening it, for fear that he was getting hate mail from Europe. He finally opened it while on yard call.

August 1990

5 August 1990

Hi Jane,

It was more than nice to hear from you. How are you and your love ones at this time? Hopefully, all of you are enjoying the wonders of life. For myself, I wish I was anywhere beside here.

I still don't know what's taken so long with the picture. The last time, it only took eight days but you will get one.

I haven't been doing too much lately. I been trying to get over to the hospital about my eyes. I think I'm going to need glasses. For a long time, I went without using the light in my cell.

You ask about how it is when one of us get our case turn down. For some, it's not hard because their case might not be use in order for the guy case to get turn down. What I'm saying, is that my case might be use in four or five other case. What it all come down to, is one person case can get other people case turn down – that's why we feel it so hard. Like, right now, Fred is the only one that have a date, but others is going to follow. The lawyers I have, I wish I would have had them at first – things would have been different. I do think that things is going to get a lil better for me, I just got to wait and see.

Here, where I am, it got 34 men. It got a few more but they are on court order. Most of them that go on court order don't come back with the death penalty. I'll be glad when I go. Like I said, these same faces get next to me. It have been a long time, and to find evidence, it's going to be hard.

Since I been here, I have learn that the grandparent wasn't even at home, and she was there by herself. The mother, she said she was in one place but was in another one. A lot have come up or I would definitely have been dead by now. You know, it's only about seven people that's alive from 1984 when I came here. Things had gotten hot around here in 1987. Each year that past, somebody was on their way out.

Jane, my life wasn't easy. I got some story to tell that's something else. That's why I told you that I don't feel bad about being here for something I didn't do. This penitentiary is full of people that here for something I did. I didn't live for tomorrow. During my time, I just live for that day.

I haven't talk to my lawyer about where to put my body if I get executed, but I will do so now that I'm thinking about it because I definitely don't want it here. Everyone here want their body away from here.

Yes, we do get a lot of bad letters – people write all kinda stuff to us. I wonder if they would do it if they had a family member here. I never let it get me down because there is more good people than bad.

Anyway, you ask about the weather. The summer is hot, the winter is not so cold – the lowest it get is about 22, but we still have to have coats because that is cold. What I was saying about the coats, everybody have to use the same one, so that's why most people stay in. When I go on the yard, I run to stay warm because the coats be wet with somebody else sweat. Yes, the yard is big enough for me to get a good run, even if I have to go round and round.

Yes, my father was a chauffeur until he die, and he always did work for the same people, and yes, we did things together – he was a good father. I remember when he use to fix the car and I would break it again. Working on cars, that's what I use to like to do with him. I end up working at a car lot for a while. I knew everything about cars through him.

You take it easy and say hello – and I'm sorry about my writing, my hand is hurting again.

Peace
Andrew Lee

21 August 1990

Hello Jane,

Your letter came today and as always, I'm glad to hear from you and to know that all is well. Like for myself, I'm fine but I could be better if I wasn't sitting in this cell. Like after all this time, I still haven't gotten use to being lock in for four and five days in a row, especially when it's so hot.

Did you like the card I sent? I make them better, I just haven't made one in a while, and I wanted to get it to you on time for your birthday. I make a lot of things: picture frame, jewel boxes. I'm very good at making things. Like I said, I use to make things to get the stuff I need. When I get myself back together financially wise, I'll make something for you.

My picture came back. I have to send it to another company to get some copies made. You will have one sooner or later. You know it's hard to get something done when you are lock up.

The crime I was in jail for was rape. Myself and a girl named Mary, we pull a jewellery store robbery in another town, and when we got back to Baton Rouge we went to a Motel to lay out for a while, and during the time I was asleep, she decided that she wanted everything. So what she did was took everything out of the room, and then left without her clothes on and call the police.

They didn't want to take me to jail because the owner told them we had checked in together, and there was nothing for him to suspect that something was wrong. My luck was bad that night. I was leaving out of the room when the police officer came that had arrested me before. He knew I was the (can't say what) robber, he just couldn't prove it. When they did catch up with me and I went to court, the charge was drop.

Mary, she thought I was going to catch back on her. When I saw her, I just smile and kept on going.

When I was on the run, I met a lot of people. Life was very different then because you only live for today, because tomorrow might not come.

Anyway, I use to be into fiction, non-fiction, and I loved to read poetry. Like the first time I pick up a cowboy book, I knew I was hooked because they remind me of myself – always on the run. I loved moving from place to place.

Okay, you take it easy and I hope everything was nice for your birthday.

Peace
Andrew Lee

September 1990

11 September 1990

Hi Jane,

Hopefully, you and your family is as well as can be at this time.

Your letter took a long time to get to me. It's dated for the 5th and I didn't get it until today, the 11th.

Like things haven't been going well for me. I have a very bad cold. Also my lawyer, Rebecca Hudsmith, she have quit. She is going back to her home town to work. I'm waiting to hear from Nick now, to find out who is going to take over my case. She was the best lawyer I had. I'm going to miss her deeply.

Anyway, it's one execution date set for this month on the 21st, and it's one for the next month, on the 10th. Both of them have had over five dates – Robert and Fred.

My birthday wasn't nothing to talk about. I did get to go outside that morning and thank you for thinking about me because I definitely was feeling very low. I thought of many things I could have been doing.

You sound very happy to be going back to school. I wish I was going anywhere, and I am glad you are going to use the stamps. I'll look around for some more.

How far is Italy from where you are? Do you go there when you have spare time? There's a Scotland down here but it's no place to talk about. Like Boston is a good state. I like their basketball team.

Also thank you for being concerned about me. I definitely can use the help. I wish you had a lawyer you could send.

I'm looking forward to the hearing next month. The lawyers from UCLA have been coming regularly to get our case ready. If everything works out okay, time won't be so hard around here; we will have something to do other than just sit around.

I catch this cold from not having any fresh air. It's fifteen people on this tier, and just two of us don't smoke. My two neighbours smoke like it's going out of style. It's hard to stand by the bars when they are woke.

Anyway, your son's friend definitely had a hard time being lock up. I have hard times myself. Sometime when I'm watching the news, I see people that I know. I even seen my sister, some of my old girl friends. I hate watching the news but I have to watch it so I can know what's going on.

The only newspaper that's on Death Row is Sunday, and it don't come until Monday. Anyway I'm glad that I've gotten to know you. I have a letter to look forward to. I too like hearing from you. I always think about your first letter and now I can read you letter without checking the words.

Oh, I finally got the information about my grandparent. My grandfather's real name was Donald Nash. He had to make a run for it from Mississippi, and he change it to Willie Jones. That was my father's father I'm talking about.

My picture will be in the mail, Monday. I found out they will be taking pictures, Sunday. I never did hear from the company where I was trying to get copies made. They still have my picture too.

Okay, about the poetry: I like to read it but I haven't like any kind except the inspiration poems. I wish you hadn't said that the guy's body never made it home. That put fear in my heart. I hate the thought of being left here. Like after reading the poem,[*] I felt what he felt; he wanted his home land, he wanted to be home. No one should be left in prison or a strange land.

*This was Rupert Brooke's poem, 'The Soldier'.

Okay, you ask about the food. On one shift, the food is cook, the other is not. But, to live, you must eat something. Like Monday, Wednesday, Friday, we have eggs; Tuesday, Thursday, it's pancakes; Saturday, it's sweet rolls; Sunday, it's anything. The noon and evening meals could be anything too. What I do is never ask what they got, I just let it come. The only meal I miss from not having what I want is fish – it's just on Friday, we have it here. Okay you say hello and keep yourself well, and I'll just wait here to hear from you.

Peace/Love
Andrew Lee

This cold is getting the best of me.

16 September 1990

Hello Jane,

Here is the picture. It didn't come out too good, but you can see who you have been writing to. It came out kinder blue. He said he will come back another time and take them. You will get a better one.

Anyway, how are you at this time? Hopefully everything is fine for you and your family. I'm well now. That cold I had had me feeling badly.

On the picture, the only reason why I have the towel on my hands is because the rules say the hand cuffs can't be shown on the picture. Also, I didn't know he was going to take the whole body, they usually just take the top.

Okay, the guy Fred who had a date for this month; he got a stay, Friday. Now it's just the one for next month. Also, the chaplains have put together a three day seminar for us – 18, 19, 20 – that's this week. We have it every year. Okay you say hello, and I'll await to hear from you.

Peace
Andrew Lee

28 September 1990

Hi Jane,

Your letter came today, Thursday, and as always, glad to hear from you and to know all is well. I'm fine also.

The seminar* went well. I had a very good time. I was the spokesman for our group. We were in three groups. The people that made it possible for the seminar was from Prison Fellowship, out of Washington DC. They also had a judge from Baton Rouge, along with them. He said a few words. He said that he didn't feel uncomfortable being around us, he enjoyed our company. Also, they are the ones that give our names to different organisation.

In your last letter, you mention prison support. They also have a group call Prison Justice Support. From the way they said, all of the group are made up from Prison Fellowship.

Anyway, let me say this, Fred, he have a stay. Robert, he have a Pardon Board hearing set for the eighth of next month.

Here in Louisiana, the Pardon Board is just for nothing. If they recommend for a life sentence, the Governor, he over rule them. Early this year, the Pardon Board had change Dalton Prejean death sentence to life in prison, and the Governor over rule them, and Dalton got executed. They had a Prime Minister wrote the Governor and ask him for a stay for Dalton. Lots of people from your country wrote him on behalf of Dalton. If Robert don't get a stay from the Supreme Court in the next few days, it's over for him. He was in my group at the seminar, and he knows what he is going up against.

I don't have too many privileges; one hour on the yard for three days, a TV, one hour on the hall for four days, five phone calls a month, a law book if the Inmate Counsellor bring it, store call, a radio, and that's it. They stop church call. What it all came down to is this: we are just here; like we can't

*An annual religious seminar run by prison support groups. This was the one day of the year when all the men were together.

make anything, we don't have any needles. All we got is time
with nothing to do with it. If these doors was open we can
play chess, checker, or cards, and whatever else we can play.
This tier is big enough for them to put some cabinet for a
library. I don't think all the other Death Row in the United
States is like this one. I hope something hurry up for us.

I have a book now. If you would like to have it, I'll send it
to you. You know you are full of surprises with your reading.
Have you ever read about the Civil War that stop slavery? I
also have that too, and I'll send it to you. I bet you have some
good books at your house. I wish you could send some from
your house. If you have any books that you would like to read,
and it's here on Death Row, I'll send it to you.

Okay, I'll wait to hear from you.

Peace/Love
Andrew Lee

October 1990

9 October 1990

Hi Jane,

It was so nice to hear from you, and to know that all is well for you and your family.

Anyway, you will get a better picture. I wish I would have known that the guy was going to take a whole picture – I would have fix myself up better. What you see in the back of the picture, is a poster to make the picture come out better. If I could have my own background, that would be nice, but the people that draw the background, they act like a person have a job here on Death Row.

Speaking of Death Row, Sawyer, he got a stay yesterday. The Pardon Board wanted to look over his case some more, so he will have a few more days before he know if he is going to get a definite stay or an indefinite one.

Anyway, my hair-cut – people still ask me why I keep getting my hair cut that way. Everytime I get a cut, I get it cut a lil different. The picture was taken outside of the tier gate – they don't let us take them in the cell. I wish I could because you can see then how small they are. It's just wide enough to let me to do my exercise, and it's cold in here too. Like I said this place is full of window. That's why a lot of people have bad colds here; it's nothing to stop it.

Let me say this – when one person on Death Row get a date, we all feel it. It's no telling who will be next to sit in that chair for I have out-live many. Some of them came after me.

You know, after an execution, it take weeks before anyone is himself again. Nobody have too much to say. Like before Sawyer got his stay, everybody was looking crazy. Like last week five more case was heard and no telling which out of the five will sit in the chair. It's going to be a while before anyone is really himself again.

Anyway where you are the crime rate is not bad. It's very bad in this state – rape, killing, robbery, it's always going on. But we both know, as long as there is people, something is always going to go on. We just got to face it when it come.

I was doing a lil more writing today on my book. You got my word on it that as soon as I find out who I'm going to have for a lawyer and what he think about it, I'm going to send it to you to read. You will find it very interesting, and you can share it with Chris because you and her must be very good friends.

I got half of the order back for the magazines that you order for me. Like *Secrets* and *True Experience*, they don't deal with them anymore. I took the money and order *True Experience*, so I'll be getting that and *True Story* for a year. Thank you for them.

The weather here is getting cold. It's raining outside, now. Too much rain stop us from going outside, and I don't feel right when I don't get my hour on the yard. I said it's the only time I can really feel a lil freedom. When it really get cold, these lights is going to be on all night because not too many on this tier is going to go on the yard. You know Jane, winter is the worse time of the year here, to be box in with the same people, seeing the same thing when I look out of the window. I wish I could be one of them squirrels where I can jump from tree to tree. It just get so hard sometime around here. I found out that when they have the hearing, they are just going to hear some issue on some of the things we ask for. The hearing this month is just for legal aid, and a law library, so I don't know when the hearing is going to be for the rest of the issue. I'll let you know when I find out.

I'm just going to sit here and do a lil more writing in my book. So you take it easy and say hello. Until I hear from you.

Peace
Andrew Lee

16 October 1990

Hi Jane,

Your letter came today, Tuesday, and as always, glad to hear from you and to know all is well for you and your family and friends. Hopefully, everything is still well for you all.

For myself, I'm well, and I'm happy for Sawyer. He was the one I told you about, who had the date for the 10th of this month. The Pardon Board needed more time to look into his case, and the Governor granted him a thirty day reprieve, so he won't know anything else until next month sometime. The Governor really surprise everyone here in Louisiana after what he did to Dalton, he could have given him a stay. I think he want to hold someone for the lethal injection – it become legal on the first of the year. Also, I think I told you that the Supreme Court is looking into five of our case. So far, one of the five have gotten turned down.

I think next year is going to be a hot one. It was in 1987, when eight people got executed from 7 June to 24 August, my birthday. I also had two dates that year.

Anyway, since all these cases have been coming up, things have been changing a lot around here. All the late night talking, the misunderstandings – all that is low. I guess, everyone is beginning to realise that life is short here on Death Row, and that they should come together because we are all in the same boat. Even after the seminar, everyone seem to have change. I definitely feel a change in my life. I want to thank you for coming into my life, to let me know that many more care for me as a person, not as some confined inmate.

I wrote to Helen Prejean once before. She wrote back. I never did get a chance to meet her. She use to come and visit Willie C. before he got executed in 1987. Matter of fact, everyone here on Death Row know her. Each year she be holding a rally about the death penalty. One day, it's going to be out-lawed here in Louisiana, but I wonder how many is going to sit in that chair or be injected.

It's just too lonely around here. That's why, I like to write after midnight – so I won't have to think about how lonely I am.

I wish it was possible to get some stamps in the mail because I have some books I would like to send, but I don't have the stamps to do it with. I like your interest in reading and the things you know. I'm beginning to know you like a book. Also, the maps was on time. It's funny, they let them in. Also, thanks for the picture of St Paul's. I forgot to tell you, I keep all cards. I use them to make other cards.

Thanks for the history run-down. You got to bring me up to date on the part where you were talking about the kids in India. You know, I always did feel that slavery still exist in some parts of the world. Take Africa, the way things are over there. I do believe that there are some in there. But in real life, to be lock up is slavery. A person can't never do what he want. He or she always got to be told what to do and how to do it, but that's legal slavery.

Peace/friendship always
Andrew Lee

23 October 1990

Hi Jane,

Just a few lines to let you know that I'm fine and hoping that you and all your love ones are the same. I had the book on the Civil War mail off to you today. I didn't have enough stamps to send the other one. It was $6.50 to send that small book. The other one is about four times the size of that one. When I get enough stamps to send it to you, I will.

I wrote you a letter on the 16th and I put it in my bars and went to sleep. And when I woke up, it was gone. And the lights was out. So I don't know if it was mail off.

It's starting to get cold, and these guys don't know that fresh air is good for them. These last few days have been rough for me. My window was the only one open and all the smoke come right by my cell. I ask a guy to trade cell with me but he said he like being in the back.

I got the feeling that this is going to be a long hard winter for me because these people smoke like they are going to stop making them.

Anyway, I still haven't gotten a lawyer and when I talk to Nick everything is still the same on my case. Also, the five cases that come up, nothing is being said about them. Hopefully, they will hold off until after the holidays. Nobody want an execution date hanging over their head.

Okay, I just want to let you know that I'm getting along well and that the book is on the way. So you take it easy and say hello.

Peace
Andrew Lee

29 October 1990

Hi Jane,

Your letter came Friday and as always glad to hear from you. Hopefully at this time you and your family is well as can be. For myself, I'm well. I just been keeping myself in shape and watching the football games. I'm glad that basketball is back. Also watching sports help me out a lot too.

Anyway, like I'm glad you are enjoying yourself. Like I also saw that movie *Raiders of the Lost Ark* and *Star Wars* too. Like, I watch a lot of TV myself. Some of the movies is good, some is not.

I was glad for Sawyer myself. I just hope they don't put the date back on him. Remember, he only had a thirty day reprieve. Also, I just found out that a guy name Curtis, he have a date for next month but he don't have too much to worry about now because his appeals is just starting out.

Louisiana Death Row is nothing like Texas or any other Death Row. It's not too many here that get off of Death Row alive. A few years back it had one guy die of cancer and he was getting close to being executed. And a few months ago another guy got off of Death Row and he have cancer. They sent him to another prison here in Louisiana.

Right now it's five people here that's just about out of their mind, and it's about four that don't know how to read or write. If the doors was open, where one can have the time, they can learn to read and write, but Jane, we just get a hour on the hall and during that hour we must shower, make a hot and cold water run. Being lock up for so long, when a person come out, they want to walk around for a while and don't have the time. It's one guy here with one hand. I showed him how to roll a cigarette with one hand but he didn't want to learn. I ask him if he wanted to try again but he said no.

Anyway, like thank you for thinking about us. Each and everyone of us will give anything to have a walk on them hills. Thanks for the pictures. I put myself on a horse riding up those hills.

When I had my last date, I was very paranoid. I kept thinking that the people on the tier wanted me to die. I had put my back up against the wall. For some reason, I couldn't move. I kept thinking that a month ago, the guy that was in the next cell had gotten executed. Me and him use to have some good conversation together. He knew that they was going to execute him. Before he went, like on Christmas night, he tried to get away but he couldn't get the leg cuff off fast enough. That was in 1988. His name was Wayne.

Sometime a man might feel like the whole world is against him. Really Jane, it's hard to really say how everyone take it because my neighbour, he lost his mind, and he didn't have nothing to worry about at that time because it was his first appeal, and he didn't have a date. All that the Newsman said was that his appeal was rejected.

Most of the time, the first date be for a couple of days or so. Really, it all depends on the person. I hope you can get the picture of how I'm explaining this. I want you to know how it is.

Okay, I'm going to hold back from writing the letter to *Wing of Friendship*, because we have one here called *Angolite*.* I suppose to be in the one for next month, and I'm going to send it to you. I was the spokesman from our group. The people from the prison magazine was there for the seminar – in it. It's going to be a picture of everyone that was at the seminar. It come out every month. You can get them. They are $12.00 a year. We don't have to pay for them, just the free people. What I'm going to do, is when I get the money order, I'll order them for you, okay?

Anyway, you ask if I have a heater in my cell. No, it's no heater, and it get more colder on this tier than it be on the outside. I told you, this place is nothing but big window. At times it get so cold I can see my breath. It don't get next to me when I'm running the yard or running the hall. I'm in good, good shape. I can run the yard for my whole hour. I take multiple vitamins twice a day; one in the morning and one at night, so it's nothing for me to run like I do. When it rain and we don't go out, I do my running on the hall. We don't lose our yard call. What they do is set it for another day when it's not raining.

I'm going to close now so I can get a lil rest for yard call. So you take it easy and say hello, and I'll await to hear from you.

Peace
Andrew Lee

*Louisiana State Penitentiary's bi-monthly magazine. The editorial board is made up of prisoners themselves.

November 1990

6 November 1990

Hi Jane,

Both of your letters came today, Monday. I definitely liked the card. That was the first one I ever seen like that. Also, I was glad to hear that all is well for you and your family, and your friends too. Like for myself, I haven't been doing too much – just trying to hold on for one more day.

Another Major have taken over. He started this morning, so I don't know if he is worser or what. I have just about learn to put up with everything that go on around here.

Anyway, I hope you liked the book, and I'll be looking for the ones you send. Any books that you send, I'll read them. I'm going to need something to pass the winter with.

It was kinda cold this morning, and it's going to be a lil colder tomorrow morning. All of us here is getting ready for a cold winter this year. We learn that last year, that it's colder in than out.

No one is thinking about the Christmas holidays too much because a few people might have execution dates. When a case get turn down, it be within 30 to 45 days before they get a day. I know it's one for this month, and Sawyer, he can get another date after the 8th of this. I definitely was hoping that no one will have one because I had gotten turn down on 24 December in '87. My whole lil world had fallen down on me that day. I remember saying, 'Why, why at this time?' You know, during a holiday it should be a time when one should be able to just relax and not have to worry about dying. Don't get me wrong now, I'm not afraid to go – it's just that no one wants to know when. And there is the ones that can't stand to know they have one.

I wish that you were able to just talk to some of these guys here. Some are very nice, some are so-so, some that just don't care. It's so many different attitudes around here. For, to say that we are all in the same boat, when I first came here I couldn't understand why it was like that. But, after a while I did – no one want anyone to be close to them because at any time they might be executed. And being around the same person, day in day out, makes a person mad.

I wish I could explain better what I have to go through each day. I must admit that at times, I don't know if I'm going or coming. I miss doing the things I use to do. I think of you and your friends doing all the wonderful things that life has to offer. I wonder what it would be like to be with friends again, Jane. It's been a long time since I talk to anyone that I know. I don't know if the people that I know is still alive. It hurt to just see people and don't know any of them.

I'm the only person here on Death Row that's from Baton Rouge. And it's one guy from New York. I can see the hurt in his face to be so far away from home and don't know anyone. It would be nice if I can have someone that I know who I can go back to the good times with. I have seen a few people I know on the News. You know, I'm lonely right now just to think about having a talk with someone I know. Really, it's hard for me to go on without seeing a face I know. But I just go on. I know one day, it's going to be over – things just look bad right now.

I like to thank you for being you. I thank the Lord for letting you pick up that pen and started writing to me. You know, the first letter that I receive from you, I was out on the yard. I remember trying to figure out the words. Your writing don't look funny to me any more. Every now and then, I might have trouble with one or two words. I enjoy writing to you. I feel like you are a very good friend. I been found myself when I can't wait to hear from you. I guess it come from being so lonely, and listening to the same talk and doing the same thing everyday. Your letter always have something you did, or going to do. Your life is full of hope and fun. My life is hard and sad. When I hear from you, it's like being there, to have something different to think about.

Anyway, I'm glad to know that you are a part of Amnesty International. They need more people like you and your friends. It's people like you that is going to get rid of the death penalty. I feel it that you are a very wonderful person. A lot of people wouldn't write a condemn man here unless it was something bad. But we know it's good people all over the world.

I think it's nice that all of you send the cards. Like, it's some people here on the Row, that don't get a card for Christmas. Anyway, thanks for the name of that lady. She haven't come this way. Some people came but they wasn't from Amnesty International. Sometime, they let people come down the tier just to see what it's like on Death Row. Some people from London was here. They talk with some people. I couldn't talk to them because I don't have a lawyer. They took a lot of pictures of the tier. They were from the BBC TV.

Thanks for the info on the India people. Life could be hard. I just hope for the day that a lot more people like you will become a part of Amnesty International, and make the world a better place to live; where everyone will have a better chance to live a long and happy life.

If I were close, I can teach you Pig Latin. It's best that way because I can't spell some of the stuff. I learn how just by listening to other people. There is some other language around here that I understand and can't speak but a few words of it. I have heard that there is over 100 different kind of language. I bet it would be funny to be in a room where everybody speak a different language. Like I use to have a girl friend – her family couldn't speak or hear. It didn't take me long to learn sign language. I wonder what happen to them.

Anyway, the Louisiana football team is the New Orleans Saints. My team is the Philadelphia Eagles. Like, they won yesterday. They are 4 – 4 now. The Saints are 3 – 5. Neither team is doing good this year. Like, I know they show one game over there. I didn't know that they were still showing them. If I remember right, I think it was the first or second game of pre-season that was played in London.

Do you get a chance to see basketball on TV? I like the Chicago Bulls – they are losing 0 – 2.

I never gotten around to watching *Dynasty*, and the book she wrote, they made a movie out of it call *Lucky*. Matter of fact, I never watch a movie that Joan Collins was in. I keep away from soap opera, love story – that just add on to going crazy around here.

Okay, you say hello, and have fun for both of us, and I'll await to hear from you.

Peace/Friendship
Andrew Lee

18 November 1990

Hi Jane,

Just a few lines to let you know that all is well and that your letter came Friday. And, as always, glad to hear from you and to know that all is well for you, and your family. And hopefully, all will be well when you get this letter.

The copy of the *Angolite* haven't made it to us yet. Like, we are the last one to get it. Whenever I get it to you you will find it very interesting. It always have something about Death Row in it.

The people from that London TV station had a phone conversation with the guy in the next cell from me. When they were here, they didn't have the time to talk to him so they had it fix so that they could while they were in Washington DC.

Also, the Supreme Court will be hearing his case and the Ward case on the 29th of this month. Jane, right now the court is looking into over 10 cases. The last time they did that, in one year, 8 people got executed in less than 3 months. And I think I told you that they are going to start using lethal injection. It's in effect at the 1st of the year. And yes, it do get next to most of us when all them cases start coming up. It's some here that were around for 1987 – it a was sad time then.

Lately I haven't been sleeping too well because I feel it that my case is coming up soon. I wouldn't be feeling like this if the Perry case wouldn't have come up. It's bad to have the same judge with someone else. I know that judge have me on his mind. I do hope that the judge rule in his favour because Perry, he's not right in the head. They say he was like that before he killed five members of his family.

I have been thinking about all of you. I wish I could just have a day of freedom. Last week, a guy went on a court order, and he is still talking about what all he seen. The guy been here for years. I'm hoping that I can go back to court. I haven't been outside of this gate but once since we move up here. That was on 7 November last year. We use to take a ride to the hospital, but now, we just go upstairs. We are, what you might call, box in.

I have a spiritual advisor who come to say a prayer with me every now and then. The most any of us will see a spiritual advisor, is when we have a date.

It's good to know that so many people is starting to get together to help get rid of this death penalty. We need more people like you all here in Louisiana. People here be more than happy when someone get executed – it's like a holiday. If you were here for just one, you wouldn't believe that people can be so happy about an execution.

About Halloween, it's mostly a child holiday. Kids just go from door to door saying trick or treat and get candy, and they have on disguises. We have a Holiday for this month; Thanksgiving Day. It was said that the pilgrims gave thanks to God for their survival and the bird that they had cooked, which was a turkey. So, every fourth Thursday of November, everybody in America cook turkey. And for Christmas – not everybody celebrate it. For some, their religion is against it.

The hearing for the issue that we have been asking for is on the 30th of this month. We don't expect to get all, but we should get something. And I still haven't gotten a lawyer but it shouldn't be too much longer before I do.

I don't play too much basketball – it's no fun playing by myself. When I was on the outside, I didn't play too much then, either. If I wanted to play here, I wouldn't have the time to do so because I use my hour to run the yard. Every now and then, I might walk around the yard for half an hour. I feel like, if I miss a couple of days from not running the yard, I might get lazy. Most of the guy on this tier is.

Okay, like take it easy and definitely have a nice weekend. And, I'll wait to hear from you.

Peace/Friendship
Andrew Lee

25 November 1990

Hi Jane,

Just a few lines to let you know that I'm well, and that I was just sitting here thinking of you and your family. Hopefully, all is well.

I still haven't gotten a lawyer, and Sawyer, he still have the date for the 8th of next month. He is getting very worried. On the 1st, he won't be able to go on the yard anymore. They put a person in confinement seven days before the date. When Dalton got executed, he was lock on a tier by himself. That was the worst thing they could have did, but they say he want it that way. I think too that it was for the best – that's a very good way for one to have a peace of mind.

Anyway, I just wanted you to know that I was thinking about you, and like the books never came – they might come tomorrow. We didn't have mail call 21, 22, 23. They had stop the mail because of the Thanksgiving Holiday.

Okay, you take it easy and say hello. I'll await to hear from you.

Peace/Friendship
Andrew Lee

26 November 1990
27 November 1990

Hello Jane,

Your letter came today, Monday, and I'm always glad to hear from you. I had wrote you a few lines last night, letting you know I was thinking of you. Anyway, I hope this letter finds you and your family in the very best of health. For myself, I'm fine. I just hope I get to go outside tomorrow. I haven't been outside since Thursday. They are putting the razor wire up higher so the balls won't burst.

Remember I told you why they don't let the stamps in – they don't want nothing to come in the mail that they sell in the store here. We use to get them. I think Louisiana Death Row is the one that can't get them in the mail. I wish I could get them. I have a book I like for you to read.

Before I go on, the Major that's here now, he don't mess with anyone, everything is back the way it was. The man, he just wanted to let people know he had the power to mess over other people, and I must say he did a good job of doing it.

You ask about Tommy's case. I saw him a week ago on the yard. He was getting a new trial. The next time I see him, I'll let him know about his pen-friend. You know Jane, you and your friends is changing the lives of many people here on Death Row. I see people writing that I haven't seen writing before.

It's good to know that people care. I thank you for being my friend. You have definitely brought new hope to me. Your letters and thoughts mean a lot to me. I learn something new each time I hear from you. I had already heard about the issue in South Africa. I heard it on the news last week. It is a shame that the world is still like that. Some day, people is going to realise that we must live as one. At one time, it was hard for people to get along with each other right here on Death Row. I couldn't believe it at first. Then, when all the execution started, a big change came over everyone; everyone realise that he could be next. Yes, it is hard to be here with the thought of being next. With New Year coming in it's going to be hard on a lot of us. Every year somebody die in the chair and with Sawyer, that have the date, he might go before the year is out. I hate to think about next month.

I wrote Jan Arriens. I told him if he want to, he could write what I told him. Also, I told him that you were my friend. The *Angolite* came today – we won't be in there until the next issue. This issue is about the death penalty. You will get it okay. Also, Spanish is one of the language here. I speak enough to get by with. I heard that it was over a hundred languages. I didn't know they had that many.

I guess you do have a hard time at school with all them kids from everywhere. I wish I could be there. I could use some out of this place. Yes, it do get cold in here. The heater, it work, but like I told you, it don't do any good because of all the window – it's a big one in front of every cell, and it's a big one at the end of the hall. It be cold to set up sometimes. For our clothes, we have to buy them our self. The only clothes the prison issue is under-shorts, T-shirts, and one sweat shirt. We have to buy sweat pants, PJ's, hats, all our winter stuff we have to get. I told you about Thanksgiving in my last letter, I bet you had to laugh at me – I forgot Thanksgiving is everywhere.

I started writing this letter last night. I had the feel I was going to get a letter today (Tuesday) from you so I waited for an hour and it came. It's Tuesday evening now. Thanks for the other card. Also, I didn't hear about the guy in Virginia – a lot of the stuff about the death penalty I don't hear about.

I only get the newspaper on Sunday, and the TV news, they mostly just speak of the Louisiana death penalty. I hope he didn't get executed.

You know, everytime a state have an execution, another state try to do the same. Like, Louisiana is the third state with the most executions. Texas is first, and Florida, the second.

Yes, I use to ride horses. I live in the country for a long time. Where that place is on the card, I can just get lost there. I wish I would have known that England was that nice. If I ever get out of this, I would like to visit there.

I did know about the 6 to 8 weeks on the magazine – that is a very long time to wait, especially with the winter in. Like, I should start getting them in a couple weeks.

Also, I hope that you keep on having all those wonderful times. When do you have time to rest? You are a very busy lady. Is it anywhere you like to go as a favourite place?

You know, I wonder if I'll ever be able to go anywhere the way the courts are. I don't know. I haven't heard anything else on my case. Like sometime, it might be a couple of years. At one time, it use to be every six months – that was when I first came here, and I don't like to think too much about it. Like I told you, I have had 7 dates and the next could be my last. My next step could be for the Pardon Board when it do come up, and my last two dates was too close for comfort.

Sometime before Christmas, we are taken pictures and you will get a better one, okay? And I will have the *Angolite* order for you – then you will know all about the situation here.

I'll let you know when the order come but in the meantime, you take it easy and say hello to all, and I definitely appreciate everything you are doing for me. Keep yourself well and happy.

Peace and friendship
Andrew Lee

December 1990

Hi Jane,

I received your 25 November letter, Friday. I couldn't answer back over the weekend because I didn't have any stamps – the ones I had, I use them to answer the people that send the cards from your way. Also, I got three more cards, Friday. I didn't answer them because of the stamps. Also, the one from Cynthia, she said you and her are friends, the one from Dee (she said she is your secretary) and I got one from a name I couldn't make out but I think it's Rowan. Like say hello and tell them that I'm sorry that I wasn't able to send a thank you note, and hopefully that I will soon.

Also, about *Angolite*, you are going to have to order it. The one I have here, I'm holding it for you until I get the stamps. This one is very interesting – it tell you all about the electric chair – how the body be burn. It got pictures. I would cut them out and send with this letter but it got the writing and I don't want to mess that up. Also, they got the hearing with the Pardon Board that Sawyer had. Oh, and found out today that Sawyer's date is for the 14th and not the 8th, and a guy name Tyrone, he got a date for the 11th. Like, the 8th is for another hearing for him.

Jane, right now everyone is trying not to think about what might happen in a few days but it's starting to show, and it get worse when it get within the last few days because they start checking to see if the chair work, and sometime the lights will go out. Anyway, I don't want to start thinking about it.

It's odd that you would say about learning about the world from TV and radio and not being a part of it. I had been thinking about that for a long time. Since I started corresponding with you, I have been thinking more about it. The places you tell me about – that beautiful valley, the mountains, hills – I just let my mind wander. I feel so free.

Jane, you are doing the right thing. Enjoy the freedom you got for when I hear from you, I enjoy it too. Okay, I just wanted to say that I thank you for being my friend. Also, I hope you got the check back – it was send back on the 28th. I send you the paper in my last letter, along with the order. Again, if my next letter be late, it would only mean that I haven't got any stamps. So, you stay well and always enjoy yourself.

Peace/Friendship
Andrew Lee

10 December 1990

Hi Jane,

Your letter came today, Monday, and as always, glad to hear from you, and to know that all is well.

Anyway, a lawyer came up, Thursday and told me that the DA is getting set to bring my case up. If he do this month, I'll be getting a date sometime next month. Also the guy from the Loyola Death Penalty Resource Center is going to take over my case – his name is Nick Trenticosta. The only thing I hate about it is that he is working with five other death cases and the way it is, all six might come up at the same time.

Let me say this, I'm not going to let it get me down when they set the date on me. I been prepare myself for this. My chance is half and half. I'm just glad that I got to know you.

I saw Sawyer, Friday, when they were moving him in the first holding cell. He is still waiting to hear about the ruling on his case. I just hope and pray that he get a stay. Right now, no one is saying too much – it's just the thought that Sawyer might get executed. This is really hard times for us. After an execution, it be months before things start getting back in order. When I saw Sawyer, Friday, I saw the hurt in his eye. I knew what he was thinking – I was like that before. The day pass fast when a date is set.

Anyway, I read it in the newspaper about the killing in El Salvador – the soldier are going to stand trial for that. Also, I don't know how any of the cases that come up is turn out. No one talk about their case. Most of the time, a guy don't say when they have a date until it come on the news. It's better that way because one person is another worry here. You know, since 1983 to 1990, 1986 and 1989 was the only two years that no one got executed. In 1983 (1), 5 in 1984, 1 in 1985, 8 in 1987, 3 in 1988 and 1 in 1990. I was here for 14 executions. It's funny I didn't go crazy. I hope I can get off of Death Row before anymore happen.

I liked the two books you send. The guy down the hall, he liked them too. I'll let you know when I get the other two, and I'll be looking for the pictures. Hopefully, my next letter will have good news about Sawyer.

Peace/Friendship
Andrew Lee

16 December 1990

Hi Jane,

How are you at this time? Hopefully, all is well.

Your letter came, Friday, and it didn't find me too well. I was getting down watching the news, and they were talking about a murder/suicide that had just taken place and when they gave out the address, I knew it was my sister. Her husband killed her and then he took his self out. It felt funny to be seeing my family on TV. It had been a long time since

I seen any of them. By she being my sister, I can request to go to the funeral and wake but I want to remember her from the way I last seen her. Also, if they want me to come, all they got to do is call. You know Jane, it's funny, but I feel like a stranger to them. The pictures I have is five and six years old. I wouldn't even know what to say.

Anyway, I was trying to think back to the last time I saw her. It should be close to five years. Matter of fact, from 1976 until now, I don't think I saw her ten times. You know, I really wish I was close to my family. I guess one day life might take a turn for me and I'll give them time to know me. Just to think about her make me feel sad because she is dead and the only thing we knew about each other were that we were brother and sister.

As soon as I get the typewriter, I'm going to start typing my stuff up. With the date I'll be getting, I want to have it all ready. I have a fifty-fifty chance, and your letters is giving me a lot of hope. Since I been writing to you, the thought of dying in the electric chair don't cross my mind too much because I have a lot to think about when you write. With your letters, I can put myself on a hill, I can run wild on an island, I can take my mind completely out of this place. It's good that I'm writing to you – I don't have to feel lost all the time.

Anyway, BBC TV have been back up here. I thought they were going to come while Sawyer had that date. The next time they come, I might get a chance to talk to them. I was on the yard one time talking to a guy when they said they were from a TV station. I didn't know at the time that it was the BBC – that was about a year ago.

Okay, I'm just going to lay here and keep my thoughts together. Jane, you and your family have a wonderful time for Christmas. Take care, okay?

Peace and Friendship
Andrew Lee

Bury My Heart at Wounded Knee was the best I ever read.

18 December 1990

Hi Jane,

Your letters of the 10th and 11th came today, Tuesday. I was getting ready to write and let you know that I had gotten the western book.

Anyway, I hope at this time all is going well for you and your family, and that you are set for the holidays. For myself, I'm fine. I thought maybe that I was going to hear from my family but all I found out is that they are going to have the wake and the funeral Wednesday and Thursday. Hopefully, I'll get a chance to talk to them then. I'm not going to let it get me down. Being on Death Row, something like that can drive a person crazy. I have seen too many people go crazy behind lil things. Just the thought of being here could break a man down.

I check around to see if any of the three guys on my tier wanted to hear from someone but they say no. They have good understanding but you would have to see them to judge them. They have build a wall between their self and other people. My neighbour, it's hard to say about him. Somedays he is right, somedays he is not. Really, they have a lot of people here that have builded walls between their self and others. Remember, I told you that no one like to get too friendly with anyone here – it's no telling when you or that person might get a date. Everyone try to avoid hardship.

You know Jane, it's every now and then a misunderstanding might come up, for we try our best to get around any kind of unnecessary pressure. For what you and your friends are doing, it's definitely a big relief on a lot of us. Like, when your friends send me the cards, I was more than surprise. I must admit, when I was sending thanks, I didn't know what to say.

The stamps I use was the ones that came with the cards they gave us. They give us 14 Christmas cards, and then they gave us a few more. And guess what I straight out forgot if I put a card in one of your letters for Chris, so I'm enclosing one in this letter.

The weather here is getting colder but it never get where it should snow. I can only remember two times that it had snowed in this part of Louisiana – in the upper part it do. Also, I heard about that guy, Brandley. Like, they had a guy here, name Novell. He got off of Death Row but he had another charge and they gave him five years flat. He was here for about a year.

Anyway, don't send anymore books, I'll send you the order for some because the amount you pay for the western book and for to have it send to me, I could have gotten 10 or 11 books. Like, the books is far less than where you are.

Have lots of fun over the holidays and say hello to all.

Your Friend
Andrew Lee

MERRY XMAS

January 1991

1 January   I'm starting out the New Year with 1 sister less. She was killed by her husband on 12 December 1990. I was watching the news when it came up. Also they had yard call. It was nice to be outside.

1 January 1991

Hi Jane,

Your letter of 15 December was very late getting to me. They had already stop the mail for the holidays. I'm glad that you did get a chance to see the building that I'm in. If only you could have seen the part where I'm at. It's nothing but another building across the yard.

I did have my hands out side of the bars when they were filming the tier.* They even came on the tier and looked around. Well, everyone do that. Some say they were told that we were hard to look at but that's not true. Anyway, they might be coming back again.

I found out that I have a date for 25 February 1991. I won't know until tomorrow what steps they are going to take. The lady who work there, she call up here for me to call the office. All she was able to tell me was that she had just gotten the call from the DA saying that a warrant had been sign for my execution, and that my lawyer wasn't in. They always try to

This was for a BBC documentary called The Last Supper *about prisoners' meals chosen as their last food before execution. I had seen this by chance while writing Christmas cards. It was my first view of the inside of Death Row at Angola. All you could see of the men on the tier was their hands hanging outside the bars of their cells.*

call first when a date is set because they don't want it to come as a surprise. As you know, some people react pretty badly. They expect a person to sign their own Death Warrant. I have sign seven of them.

Anyway I want you to know that I wasn't surprise or shock when I receive the call. I had the feeling that it was coming. I thought it was going to be for this month. Okay, I must say this; I have a fifty fifty chance of getting off Death Row so it could go either way for me. I'm glad of one thing, that I did get a chance to learn about you and your home land. You know it's funny how a person can come to know some of the nicest people that they have never seen before.

Before you started writing, I was beginning to wonder if it was anything beside prison talk that I was going to know about for the rest of my life. I ask a guy the other day how he felt about hearing the same thing every day. He said, 'That's why I keep my headphone on, it's driving me crazy.'

I haven't told anyone that I have a date. I don't want anyone looking at me with their sad eyes. I just want to go on just like I been. No one will find out until about two weeks before the date.

I can imagine how it's going to be this time. Like today, a new DA is taking over and I know he is going to try his best by his just coming in, but I won't let it get me down. Anyway, like the typewriter came, Thursday. The radio, it wasn't in stock. They are going to send it as soon as it is in stock again. Also, the magazines started coming. Thank you very much.

Anyway, I definitely hope that all went well for you and your family and friends for the holidays, and that you received lots of wonderful gifts. I did get some fruits and a yard call.

Thanks again for being so kind.

Peace/Friendship
Andrew Lee

2 January 1991

Hi Jane,

Just to let you know what my lawyer had to say today. The first issues they are going to use is the one on how had the body be burned after an execution. They are going to hold the hearing on that sometime this month. If I don't get a stay from that then they are going back to some of the issue I had before. As of now, if they just happen to rule for the issue, it's a good chance for a lot of us to get off of Death Row. I was supposed to meet my lawyer tomorrow but they call back and said that they won't be coming until Monday. I'll have to give you the whole run down then. If it come down to the Pardon Board again, a lawyer named Michelle Fournet, she might represent me. She was going to do so the last time but I had gotten a stay a couple of days before.

Also, just a few minutes ago, I received the three books. Thanks very much for sending them. The one with the pictures, *A Journey through Wales*, it's on time. It's the best book I had in years. I would love to visit that Carreg Cennen castle, that's sitting on that mountain. Your home land is something else. Tonight, I'll be in your part of the world. Like, a guy was on the hall and the first thing he ask me, 'Let me look at it tonight.' Also, another guy that write over there, he would like to have one of their maps that you send to me. Okay, thanks again for the books and for your kindness. You really put me out of this place with that book.

Peace/Friendship
Andrew Lee

3 January 1991

Hi Jane,

Your letter of 23 December arrived today, Thursday. It's five days over due. Your letters usually take from four to five days to get here. The holidays had the mail late like that. I was wondering if you had gotten all of my letters.

Anyway, thanks for the pictures and the article by Vick Roberts. His thoughts are something like mine. When he said the walls of my conscious seem to close in on me and make me inelastic. It all makes life without meaning, life without purpose. In fact, no life at all. I wrote this.

A man without hope
Is a man without a dream.
And without a dream
A man have no purpose.
For my life here
I live without the thought of a tomorrow
Now and today is what I must justify with.
For if I try to think of a tomorrow,
It only come down to one thing –
Sad, lonely and without a purpose.

I had wrote that for a lady name Sarah Ambrose. She wanted to read it at the church she go to. Like, I had a date then. I never knew if she read it to the people at the church.

Anyway, it was nice to hear from you again and to know that all was well for the holidays. Hopefully, all your friends had a wonderful time too. And yes, I enjoyed reading *Bury My Heart at Wounded Knee*. In fact, it's been in the newspaper for the one hundred anniversary. The paper say that it was over four hundred people killed there. It was a very sad book to read. Those people lost everything for being kind. Just thinking about it makes me sad.

In one of my letters I had told you that Sawyer had gotten a stay. I haven't seen him but I can hear him – he sound happy. I think you can send a tape letter if you have it mailed from a church or a store because some of the guys get sermons that was taped at church. I won't be able to send one because we can't have a tape player with a recorder.

Also, I didn't get to go to the wake or the funeral. I didn't
let it get me down. Okay, a few minutes ago the issue about
the electric came on the news. They set the hearing back until
a expert come out and check the condition of the chair, and
then they are going to rule on it. I can get a stay if they set it
back until after the 25th of next month. I'll let you know
when. Okay, you take it easy and say hello, and I'll await to
hear from you.

Peace/Friendship
Andrew Lee

7 January   11.52 a.m. Came out first for my shower. My lawyer
suppose to come at 10 a.m. It's 1.22 p.m. The Classification Officer
just brought me the Death Warrant. I had been expecting it since
last month. The mail was passed out. A letter from Jane. 4.30 p.m.
callout by lawyers. I didn't have time to find out what they are
going to do. They want me to call tomorrow, Sarah (Ottinger) and
Neal (Walker). Been up all day, but I must stay awake so that I can
watch the news.

7 January 1991

Hello Jane,

Your letter of 29 December arrived today, Monday.

While I was waiting to see my lawyer today, they came and
brought me a copy of the Death Warrant to sign. I felt very
funny signing it. I'm still feeling funny about that. I don't
recall if I ever send you a copy of the warrant, so I'm sending
this one to you.

Okay, I forgot to say in my last letter how big and beautiful
your house is. Like, how many rooms do you have? Do you
live there a lot by yourself? Just to think about being in that
big house by myself have me feeling funny. Like, I been in

this cell so long, two rooms will be too much for me.

Don't think I'm letting this date get me down. I have gotten over that part. At one time, I might have been thinking about it, but since you have been writing to me with all those new things to think about, everything just seem different for me. You really change my life. I use to get disgusted real fast just looking at the same faces and hearing the same things. Now, I just turn my back and think about running over one of them hills, or going into one of them castles.

Anyway, my sister had four boys and one girl – from 14 to 23. All everyone know is that he just did it. Some say he wasn't supposed to be there. Like, one day I might learn the truth. Okay, you take care of yourself and say hello to Chris and all of your friends, and I'll just lay here and think of times to come. Thanks again for coming into my life. I'll let you know if anyone want to hear from someone.

Peace/Friendship
Andrew Lee

8 January   Woke up this morning to pancakes. Was feeling pretty good. Talked with Jackson for a while. He said someone wrote a letter on him to the Captain. He was hot under the collar. 10.05 a.m. Woke up to beef stew. Wasn't cooked all the way. 11.20 a.m. Just finished talking to my lawyer. This date is more serious than the last two. They are trying to get Michelle Fournet to hold the Pardon Board hearing for me.

12 January   I woke up to sweetrolls and I had an urge to listen to some music. It's almost 7 a.m. and Jackson is clearing up. Went to the store. The rest of the day was so-so. I told Tony that I didn't have much to go on my case. Like, I'm not letting this date get me down. Made a deal with Chinee for a headset cord. Gave him a headset cord and he gave me his yellow cup, so that I might feel guilty about holding out on my headset. Tony told his mother and sister about my date. Just finished beating Chinee at dominoes.

14 January 1991

Hi Jane,

How are you at this time? Hopefully, you and your family are enjoying yourselves. For myself I'm just letting the days go by. Like, they are passing faster since I have this execution date. Anyway, I did get the picture of you and Chris. I would have wrote back last night but I thought that I was going to get a letter from you today but I didn't.

I started out the new year writing two copies of my diary – one of my regular. And the second, I name it count down to 25 February. It's yours even if I get a stay. The rest of the stuff you will know next month how it's going to be worked out. Oh, don't misunderstand it now, both copies are the same. I made it for you. It's just to let you know how life is for a man with a Death Warrant signed on him. I did get the radio – it's a big help. Thank you again. Okay, I hope I didn't shock you with the news about the date and the copy of the Death Warrant. I didn't mean to bring you down about it. Okay, the next day my spiritual advisor was asking me for the copy of the warrant. If you can get a copy made for her, it would be very much appreciated. I don't like to think about them myself.

Okay, thanks again for being my friend and say hello to Chris and all of your friends for me. Take it easy and stay well and I'll do the same until I hear from you.

Peace
Your friend,
Andrew Lee

If you could find a store there to send me a pair of gloves – 'M', no lining on the inside, just regular, okay?

15 January It's 6.15 a.m. and I'm wondering if Bush is going to start the war like he said. I'll know later today. Been wondering why he get it for the 15th knowing it's Martin Luther King's birthday. It's 11 a.m. – just been told that I had a lawyer call. Few minutes later I went out. Her name is Debra. From what I can tell she is very nice. We talked about all different things that happened in my past life. I would like to see her again. 12.10 p.m. Just came back. Made a deal with Shorty about the watch I had gotten from Toothpick this morning. Curtis still thinks that the crackers and meat I gave him caused his face to swell on the right side. Also, I asked Tony if he wanted to read my diary. Oh! A cup of water fell on me while I was visiting with Debra. Sgt W—— just brought the mail – a letter from Jane, my favourite person. Every time she writes, she brings me out of this prison. Called my mother tonight. She was fine except that she is still hurting over the death of my sister. It's good to talk to her after so long. She told me she knew I had a date. My sister said she didn't tell her. She didn't tell me how she found out. I'm going to have to start to get closer to my family. My mother is 65 yrs old and her eyes are going bad on her. She said that if she could get someone to bring her she will come and see me Saturday.

16 January   Wondering if there is going to be a war. Woke up at 5.55 a.m. to grits and eggs. My mouth is still sore. I cut the gum on a chicken leg. For some reason I think it's going to be a good day. It might be because I have the thought of going out on the yard. Anyway, it's funny, my neighbour hasn't been talking to himself lately, but Welcome is at it this morning, talking to his toilet again. He call it Dianne like he is saying: 'Get out – I don't need you any more.' 6.42 a.m. Big Foot Jackson just brought the mop and broom. Toothpick was with him. I haven't heard anything about a war starting. Well, my neighbour, Albert, he has started back talking to himself. I thought something had gone wrong with him. They just passed out the mail. I didn't get anything. Had yard call today. It was nice to be in the fresh air again. I was playing dominoes with Chinee when it came across the news that the war had started. 5.40 p.m. I wonder how many is going to die. It's 12.25 a.m.

17 January   I guess I'll end the night watching the news to see if they are going to fight back. So far just the USA is doing so. Woke up this morning to oatmeal and bacon. Couldn't enjoy it because my mouth is still sore from Monday. Still not sure what caused it. It's 6.08 a.m. I need to take a long nap. I have to wait for the mop and broom. Also, the thought of having an execution date is coming through to me. I'm wondering this morning if I'll get a stay. I can't think of any issue they haven't used. That judge that was on my case, all he did was turn down the issue I had. Went on the yard today and had a long talk with Bob. He was saying how much he believed in the coming of the Lord. They just brought the mail. Letter from Jane and the money order she sent. Also Carol wrote and letter from Bennett Brothers. Right now I'm getting ready to type Jane a letter. It's 4.01 p.m. It's 8.52 p.m. Just finished letters to Jane and Carol. Getting ready to listen to the radio. It's still on the news about the war. A while ago it came on the news that Israel was under fire. Woke up today to Sgt W——— marking down the clothes that is to go to the laundry room.

17 January 1991

Hi Jane,

How's everything at this time? Hopefully all is well.

Nothing else have change for me. Like they are just getting people together for this Pardon Board hearing. Like the Classification Officer came again today for some more information on where I lived, where I was from. I don't like it one bit for them to keep asking me the same thing over. As I told you of the dates I had before, they ask the same questions – they already have it wrote down.

I'm sorry that the people here have found out that I have a date. They are starting to put the sad eye look on me. I feel very uncomfortable when they do that. Hopefully, I don't sound down and out because I'm not. You have to see the look of them to really understand what I'm trying to say. I know they don't mean no harm, it's the look.

Jane, over the months that I have been writing to you, I have become close to you. You also made me feel very good when you said that I was like an older son. Jane, like I told you that I have a fifty-fifty chance, so think that you should prepare yourself for the worst. I hate to think about it but it's a chance that you might get a letter saying that I was dead. My lawyer, they are definitely wondering what they are going to do. Each time that I talk to them, they seem more interested in my diary than about helping me. I'm beginning to wonder about this fifty-fifty chance.

Anyway, how did you feel when you heard that the war had started? I been listening to the news since it started. I had been having the feeling that is going to be one. Hopefully, it won't last too long. I know some people over there. Anyway, say thanks to all the people that is praying for me. I hope some day that I could thank them. James from BBC had wrote Tony James a letter telling him that he was sorry that he miss from filming him.

Okay, I will keep you up with what's going on with my case. I'm going to call my lawyer tomorrow. I'll have you another letter in the mail, Monday. It don't go out on Saturday/Sunday here.

Anyway, the book about Wales – yes I definitely did enjoy it. Anyway, I was under the impression that that was just one big house. But still, being in that house with all them rooms will have me looking crazy. Also, I have heard that an animal can tell that a spirit is around. Like, what you should do is just watch the reaction of the cat.

I was listening to the news last week, and it's twenty-two thousand people here in Louisiana with AIDS. Like, it was a surprise to me to hear that it was that many cases. They didn't say how many had pass on with it. I had a magazine on AIDS. They had a lot of pictures that I couldn't stand to look at. That is a hard way to go.

You take it easy and definitely say hello to all. Hopefully you have been getting all my letters on time. Until I hear from you, you keep yourself well.

Peace/Friendship
Andrew Lee

20 January   6.40 a.m. Woke up to pancakes. Toothpick passed out the food this morning. Today may be a bad day. I say this because too much went on yesterday. Thomas, the guy I had a few words with, he is not in a position to start something. His right side of his body is partly paralysed. He just likes to tell loud because he knows that no-one could get next to him as everyone thinks about his handicap. Just come in from the shower room. While I was on the hall Thomas dash me down with some stuff. I didn't say nothing. I just went and took my shower. After that I call my mother and talked to her for a lil while. I was on my way back and he dash me down again. Yes, I was mad, but it wasn't nothing that I could do. The whole while he was doing it, he was trying to get the freeman's attention. I just let him talk and I act like nothing was going on. When the freeman came by the bars, diary, at this time I'm thinking a mile a minute. That guy got me really hot under the collar, like I'm really going to have to talk myself out of this one. I really want to try and kill him, but I know it's impossible. It don't make no sense to throw something back at him, and if I try to do it now they are going to send me to the Hole. But what good is it? Okay, diary, I'm going to watch a lil TV. Well, diary, I don't think he would do what he did. It's a little after 10 p.m. Thomas came out and threw some waste over me. If I'd known that he was going to pull off a cowardly act like that again, I would have had something to stop it with. Like, I'm in the Hole right now. They lock both of us up. I'm going to be here 4 to 10 days. The Disciplinary Board won't be held till Wed. as Monday is Dr King's birthday. Hopefully, I won't have to stay here 10 days. I only have 4 stamps with me. There was so much waste in my cell I had to watch where I was putting things. I don't know what time it is as I couldn't have my watch in here. All I can have is a jumpsuit, pen, paper, toothbrush, toothpaste. All I have on is this jumpsuit: no socks, no T-shirt, no undershorts. There's nothing else in this cell but a roll of paper, a blanket and 2 sheets. I won't be using this blanket because there's no telling who's been on it. Well, I'm going to try and get some rest now because tomorrow is going to be a long day. The Hole doesn't have a TV or radio. It's just what it is – a Hole.

21 January   Woke up to grits and eggs. The food was cold even. It must have gotten pretty cold in here while I was asleep because my ink don't want to write. Anyway, diary, I feel funny waking up and talking to someone new. For a moment I thought I was on the Row. I wonder what it would be like to stay for the 10 days. Part of me wants to stay, and besides, the change would be nice. But, as you know, I can't and I don't have the stamps to do so and they don't let mail come back here. It's somewhere between 10 a.m. and 12 midday. They just move me to another cell. I still don't know what unit I'm in but I'm in C-14 and this cell stinks. I thought about 10 days but I wouldn't want to stay in this stink cell. I don't know what time, but the freeman brought me some soap to clean this cell. It's smelling better than it did at first. I'll probably get out with a bad cold. Right now all I have on is a pair of home-made socks, and the vent is on because they just gas some guy down around the corner. It's all the same block. Just brought the evening meal. They've forgotten about me again. They still haven't brought me a jumpsuit and it's getting very cold in here. Just back from showering. My luck was so bad the shower got stopped up. Yes, I definitely hope I get out of here tomorrow. Camp J is the worst place I ever been in. Well, I'm going to turn in for the night. It's just so cold in here it's going to be hard for me to fall asleep.

22 January   Woke up to pancakes. The food here is very bad and I feel sick. Hopefully, this will be my last wake up time. Like, I wanted to write Jane last night, but I was just too uncomfortable. I tried to do so. I also woke up this morning wondering about the few things that I own, if they put all those messed up things in with the good stuff. I won't have any winter clothes as I already had to throw away a lot of stuff before I left. I also asked the freeman if they were going to have a Disciplinary Board court today. He said yes. Right now I don't know what time it is but it's getting colder in this cell. I tried to walk up and down the cell, but that's not doing any good. If I get up under the blanket and get caught under it, it's another write-up and I might get 10 days. Believe me, I don't want to stay here that long while it's so cold. They haven't started court yet. I don't even know if they're going to hold it. The freeman said they were, but so far nothing has happened … I'm just back from DB court. The board gave me 10 days in the Hole. I don't think I can last 10 days in here without getting some more write-ups. So, I'll probably be here until I die. Also, while I was waiting to go to court, six freemen went into a cell and beat a guy half to death and they were laughing about it. They also jumped another guy right after that. These free folks here at Camp J get away with everything they do. Well, I'm about to go in for my 3rd day in here. I wrote the warden. I wonder what the next seven days are going to be like.

22 January 1991

Hi Jane,

At this time, I'm not well at all. Sunday night, a guy came out of his cell and dash my cell with some stuff and mess up everything. Like, all the clothes I had out, my headphones – it was even on my typewriter case. I had to get rid of a lot of stuff.

I'm writing you this letter from the hold. I went to the DB court today, and they gave me ten days in the hold. It won't be until next month before you get another letter from me. I get out of the hold on the 29th. They don't let me get mail down here. I'm in a camp away from Death Row, so they are going to hold all my mail until I get back. I could write from here but I wasn't expecting to get time in the hold, so I didn't bring but four stamps.

Anyway, I did get your letter, Friday. I'll have to answer it back when I get out. I wish now that I would have brought it with me to have something to read. It's nothing in this cell but me, and it's very cold in here. This place set right side to a lake, and the air from it make it very, very cold. I get cold just to think that I have seven more days to go. Right now, my hands and feet is cold.

Also, it's very hard to get a phone call back here – I been waiting for hours to call my lawyer. They keep saying, after a while. My lawyer leave the office at five.

Anyway Jane, I'm going to write to you the first night I get out. It's going to feel funny going a whole week without a letter from you.

Thanks for those pictures that you send. I hope that you

are not as cold as I am at this time, and that you are enjoying yourself.

I'm beginning to wonder if I could last for seven more days. The food back here is bad, and it's cold. Also, I don't have nothing on but a jumpsuit – no socks, no undershorts, no T-shirt either. This place is what is a hold.

I'm going to write to the warden tonight, and hopefully, he might let me out of here. If they let me call my lawyer, I'll have him to call up here and see what he can do.

If you can see this place, you will know why I don't want to be in here – they even turn the vents on. I don't think the heaters work. I been cold since I been here. Jane, this one place I will never come back to.

The guy who throw the stuff in my cell, he did it so that he could get off of the tier, and he also knew that I couldn't get next to him. But that's okay, one day he will get something did to him, and he will think about what he did to me.

Anyway, again I must say that it's going to feel funny without a letter from you this week. I'm wondering now, did one come from you.

Okay, say hello to all of your friends, and I'll just lay here in this cold cell and think about getting out of here – and I'll have a letter in the mail to you just as soon as I get out of here.

Peace/Friendship
Andrew Lee

23 January   Just woke up to my 3rd day in the Hole. What time it is, I don't know. It was grits and eggs and I couldn't eat the grits as they weren't cooked, and the eggs were green. I ended up drinking the coffee. The guy in Cell 12 has been talking to himself all night. He is wide open at this time. Like, since I been here at Camp J I have seen so much unbelievable stuff. The guy in Cell 4, they've got him strapped to the bed with no covers. The guy in Cell 3, he sits on his bed holding his tray and looking at the wall. Diary, this place is too much. That guy in Cell 12 he is talking like someone is in the cell with him. I tell you, I'd rather be dead than lose my mind. It's a shame what those kinda people go through. Well, it's my 4th night here and these people are driving me crazy, everyone trying to talk at the same time. Like, it's so messed up back here I haven't had time to think about the date that's coming up. I guess it will really come down on me on Friday the 25th because the next 25th I could be dead. Now *that's* something to think about! But I won't let it get me down.

24 January Woke up to French toast and these fellows are wide open this morning! They talked a lot on Death Row, but being here at Camp J makes me know I'm wrong. These people do it from morning to night and Cell 12, he talk to his self more than my neighbour on the Row. Oh! And they still got the guy strapped to his bed in Cell 4. I feel sorry for him but life could be hard and it's definitely hard back here. A man could pass on just by the food. I'm drinking coffee to cut the hunger pains. They say a person can think good when he or she doesn't eat. I know that's not true because I'm forgetting how to spell small words and I can't think about nothing but the way that guy dash me down. I tell you, diary, if I could have gotten my hands on him at that time, I would have killed him. I think I'd kill him now if I could get next to him. Just too much was lost. I'm going to have to pay a couple of guys for their magazines that got messed up. Diary, I don't think I could forgive and forget this time. The act was a very cowardly one. People do things, but this was the worst. My heart hurt just to think about getting in this cell with nothing on but a jumpsuit. Like, I had to cut up a T-shirt to make a pair of socks for my feet, they were so cold. I had to use a piece to make me a towel to wash my face with. If it wasn't for that, I would have had to use paper. I'm glad I have my toothbrush and toothpaste. I do regret I don't have any stamps with me. Okay, diary, I'll get back with you later. I'm going to try and sleep as much as I can to pass this day. Woke up at 2nd meal to a spaghetti dinner. It was bad. Like, I'm finding myself eating now just to survive. These meals are not fit to eat. They've been messing over people back here at Camp J so long until they get a thrill out of it. The guards, they just pick on anyone to jump on. It's hard to describe anything back here. So much be going on. The guy in Cell 13, I started talking to him. I thought he was alright in the head, but this just came out of the crazy house. I thought something was wrong when he asked me the same thing twice last night and then asked me the same thing this morning. His name is Bobby. Diary, if I don't prepare myself for the next 5 or 6 days, I might end up losing my mind back here. Out of 13 people in this tier, four got a sound mind. I tell you, diary, it's no guarantee that I'll be right in the mind when I leave this tier. Anyway, diary, you might think me crazy for saying this, but I'll be damn glad to get back on Death Row. It's going to be real sweet to see them old faces. Hopefully, I'll never have to come back to this Hole again. I definitely didn't realise it was going to be hell. I hate writing like this when I don't know the time. But at least I know the day and the date. I just talked with the Captain. He said the guy that dashed me down wasn't in the Hole. Come to think of it, each time I came to the Hole, the other guy didn't come. The funny part about it is, I'm always in my cell. The next time, I'm going to start it and see what happens then. Well, diary, it's between 2 and 3 p.m. and they just came and got me out of the Hole. The letter I wrote to the warden, he must have thought about. Like, I'm on B-tier now. They move me and not the guy, but that's okay. But the only thing around here is that these people here don't watch the news and the TV is turned all the way up. Like, I don't know how long I'm going to last around here, but I'm going to try my best to keep away from trouble. That Hole has beat me out. It's 11.06 p.m. and I've been out of the Hole about 8 hours. I wrote my sister a letter and I tried to find a spot in this cell to make the radio work. My radio is too small to catch the station around here. I'm thinking of leaving – I was better off in the Hole. Just think, that TV is turned all the way up and a radio that don't catch any station. I'm definitely box in now. It's funny – I have to live so hard for the last few days. As you know, I could be executed next month. I know it's true now. You live hard, you die hard.

26 January   It's hard for me to sleep without a pillow but I'll get used to it. 5.41 a.m. Woke up to sweetrolls. A week ago the sweetrolls had everyone in an uproar. I wonder what the day is going to be like. They might take me out on the yard today so I'm going to rest till then. Hi, diary! 12.30 p.m. Just come off the yard. Again I was fortunate enough to be out there by myself. It felt good to be alone after so long locked in. Today I was wondering if they were going to rule in our favour about the electric chair. I've been hearing they might have a way to give everyone with the chair a lethal injection. What they are saying is that when a person got a sentence to die, the judge didn't say how. He said it was up to the State to determine how. Sawyer, he's been going to and from court since Thursday on the issue of the chair. They're supposed to make a ruling today or Monday, but most likely they're going to set it back. When I came off the yard, I called my mother. I didn't talk long. She is still worrying over my sister's death. Well, diary, it's 3.40 p.m. Sawyer just come back from the court and they turned down the issue of the electric chair. That means he'll be getting another date. It also means I'll have a harder time now. Fred has a date for next month, on the 10th. Another guy named Ford, he has one too, but it's his first. It's just me, Fred and Sawyer that's in trouble. Right now I feel bad about the ruling. Sawyer is down and out too. I knew things had turned for the worst from the way he was carrying himself and, as you know, diary, they've been after Sawyer. I wonder what the next few weeks is going to be like. A lot of people had put hope on that issue. As you know, diary, it might be the end. Okay, I just stopped to tell you this. Just finished putting my pictures in a book. I'm trying to keep myself busy. I'm not used to this – it's so much noise here. Well, it's 11.25 p.m. and I've been moving around in this cell for 2 hours trying to find a spot to get this radio to play. I put it on the bars and, so far, it's playing, but I don't know how it's going to be when the weather changes. I'm getting grey hair in my moustache. I hate to look in the mirror these days. I haven't got any in my hair. Anyway, diary, when I was told that Fred had a date, I thought he was talking about the 10th of next month, but he was talking about ten days from now. His date is for the 5th. Okay, diary, I'm going in now. I had a long day.

27 January 1991

Hi Jane,

Hopefully at this time all is well for you and your family. I'm fine myself now that I'm out of that hold. They let me out,

Thursday evening. I had wrote to the warden that night after they had given me the ten days. So I guess I must have had my record check to see that I was telling the truth about not having to write up for High Court in three years. I'm not a person to get unnecessary write-ups.

Anyway, on your 17 January letter, you said that you had wrote to me when you received the news about my date. I didn't get that letter. I had ask them about my mail. They say they had send it to me but I never did get it. I didn't even get the Sunday paper that I get. They don't pass mail out here on Saturday and Sunday, so I miss out on five days of mail. Anyway, I did get the one for last week and the week before.

Oh, I hope that you received the letter that I wrote you while I was in the hold. I didn't put the hold address on there because I knew I would have been out before your next letter. Anyway, it was definitely nice to hear from you. I was thinking about you a lot. I hate that I miss out on one of your letters.

Okay, let me tell you this: Sawyer, he went to court for four days on the hearing about the electric chair. He had thirty witnesses but the judge didn't let all of them take the stand. Yes, it was wrong but he did it. Also, the witnesses that he let take the stand: each one had witness an execution. Each one told how the chair burn a body up, how the smell of burned flesh filled the room, and the smoke. I'm going to get my spiritual advisor to get the newspaper clipping for me so that I can send it to you. They turn down the issues. Sawyer, he will be getting another date soon. Also, it's two guys that have dates: Kirkpatrick, he have one for the 5th. Ford have one; I don't know when it is. But, I know it's his first, so he don't have nothing to worry about. It's about five of us here that can't stand to have a date.

Jane, I want you to know that I'm definitely glad that you came into my life. Like yesterday, I was on the yard all by myself. I got to thinking about the book of Wales that you sent me. I had a very good vision of myself running through them woods trying to find one of them beautiful castles. I definitely would love for you to take me for a journey through Wales.

Lately, I have been thinking about it a lot. And I must admit, the last couple of days, I been thinking about what next month is going to be like. Like, right now, I feel like there will never be another day 26 for me. I went over my transcript trying to find something that's been over-look. It look bad these last seven dates that I have had. It took a lot of issue to keep me out of that chair. The 1989 stay that I got, it took up a lot. Like, for what I see, the Pardon Board is all that I have left. And I know if they do something, the Governor, he is going to side-step it. I'm going to call my lawyer tomorrow and find out if he have anything to fight with. Hopefully, he will be on the up and ups with me.

Anyway, I went to the hold for something that was unnecessary. Me and another guy was talking about the things that some sports announcers might say. And this guy Thomas, he just jump into our conversation. I told him that we were not talking to him. Then, he just start calling me all sorts of names. I didn't even pay any attention to him, I just finish watching the fight. He knew that I couldn't get to him and he couldn't get to me. I had forgotten all about it.

When I was passing by his cell that morning, he dash me down. Yes, I was hot under the collar but I just kept on walking to the shower. On my way back, he did the same thing. I went back to the shower. This time I just waited until my time was up. When he came out the night, he did the same thing. At that moment, I could have just beat his brains out. He mess up everything that I had out in my cell. I had told the guy that I wasn't going to throw nothing into his cell. I have this date to worry about. He said nothing to that. The guy in cell 5 could have said 'watch out' because the guy was right by his cell when he throw the stuff.

Jane, he mess up my sweat-pants, sweat-shirt, my headset that came with my radio, towel (it was on my typewriter case), even my toothbrush. The free man threw away everything that wasn't in my locker. I just got a blanket last night – they even throw away the tennis that I use for the yard. Jane, I must admit that it did take a lot out of me. All my stuff was thrown away. I went to the hold, I had ten days, I got moved. And, to top it all off, the guy who dash me down didn't even go to the hold. Jane, life could be hard at times but one must go on as best one can.

Thank you again for coming into my life because right now, I would be laying here trying to figure out a way to get my hands on that guy. Your letters to me each week is keeping me going. I was thinking back to the last date that I had. I didn't have nothing to keep my mind off of the date. All people kept telling me was we are getting ready for the Pardon Board, 'Are you alright?' It was like a nightmare. After reading your letters, I forget that I'm here. Jane, I just love writing to you. Like, I'm going to write to you again later today. I still haven't answer all of your letter. I didn't start this letter until after the Superbowl. I had to stop to come out for my hour on the hall too. So, I look for a letter tomorrow, okay? Your friend forever,

Love
Andrew Lee

28 January 1991

Hi Jane,

Your letter just arrived. I was getting ready to finish my first letter to you. It's nice to hear that you are enjoying yourself. I wish I could share some of the wonderful things that you be doing, like, taking the ride up and down the country-side, sharing a meal with a friend.

Jane, it's so much I would like to do but I must admit that things is looking kinder bad at this time. I may not get the chance to see Wales, but thanks to you I have a very good picture of what it would be like. Okay, today the Classification Officer came and ask me what I was going to say at the Pardon Board hearing. I wanted to tell him get on from around my cell. He didn't have any right to ask me that – it's up to me, my family, lawyer and the friends that I want to share it with. I just told him to ask my lawyer. He left then. I tell you Jane, people have a lot of nerves at times. I just hope that they will leave me along.

I guess you were wondering about the hold. It's a place where I don't want to live at. The food was unbelievable. I lost a pound or two over there. I haven't seen the guy that dash me down. He don't go on the yard. Anyway, I'm not going to let that get me down. He know in his heart that he wouldn't have did that if it was a way for me to get next to him. That's pay back for me.

Okay, let's go to your letter of 20 December. Your letter was very touching. It did make me feel sad. Life is hard here. Like a lot of time things go on here that would make you cry. Like, they got one guy here, I call Mop. He don't have anyone on the outside that's helping him. I get cigarettes for him when I can. I tried my best to get him to stop smoking but he can't. He is one of the ones that have lost their mind in many ways. He talk to himself too. I get a very sad feeling when I think about him. Suppose I would have been like that?

You know, Jane, anyone here on the Row could lose their mind. Remember in one of my early letters I told you about the worse habit a man could have here? I have seen people act up behind coffee, cigarettes, visits, simple things, and most of all, not having nothing to do. Laying around all day could get a man mad with himself. Jane it's people like you that give a condemned man new hope for a better day. I have found that it's not just lonely, sad or without a purpose to think of tomorrow. Like, I can look forward to it now. It's all because of you. Your letters take away a lonely night. I don't have to lay down sad and get sad, for tomorrow I have a purpose. The thought of a letter from you. Jane, if I go next month, it will be with a happy heart. Like, I said, I don't hold nothing against no one but like I said, I would like that journey through Wales.

Okay Jane, you take it easy and say hello, and I'll just wait to hear from you. But, as you know, I'll be writing again before the week is out.

Love/Peace
Andrew Lee

29 January 1991

Hello Jane,

I was on my way out to visit with my lawyer, when your letter of 22 December arrived. She ask me about you. I gave her your address. She said that she is going to write to you. What it is Jane, she want to know if it's possible for you to come down here for the Pardon Board hearing. They're trying to get as many people as they can.

You know, Jane, I think that I am nervous. Lately, I haven't been able to sleep. I haven't been able to get back to sleep. Right now it's 3.10 p.m. Hopefully, I'll be able to do so tonight. And, I haven't been eating right lately. Also, I miss listening to the radio. Jane, I don't know what to say about myself lately. Anyway, like I'm glad that I have you writing to me, it really help a lot. Jane, I guess we both know that it is only natural that I have some kind of nervousness. I didn't know that it was going to start so early. But don't worry I'm going to be just fine.

Okay, Nick was working with Rebecca Hudsmith when she had my case. Now, he is the top lawyer on it. Like, I don't know nothing about Sarah or Neal. I first heard about Sarah when Sawyer's case came up. I saw her twice. Neal, I saw him once. Debra, twice. All I can do is hope that Nick learn a lot during his time with Rebecca. I'll keep you in on what's happening. Okay, I'll write again soon. You take real good care of yourself and I'll await to hear from you. Say hello to all for me.

Your friend always
Andrew Lee

30 January   1.31 a.m. It's been long after 24 hrs since I slept. Oh! I got 5 books from Jane and I got the books I sent out for trade. I'll be reading for the next 2 months if I be here. That date is coming up fast. Good morning, diary. They brought breakfast at 5.49 a.m. today. I'll try and get a nap. There'll be no yard call today. It's been raining all night. I'll sleep if this old body will let me. 10.04 a.m. Just woke up to chicken, and it's cooked too! I'm going to watch the news and try for another nap. Just found out they moved Fred to the front holding cell, which they do when a person has a date. They move him to Cell 1 for a week before and during that time. If a person don't get a stay, the day before his execution they move him completely off the tier to Camp F. That's where the chair is. I hate thinking about that. Never did get a nap, but I got a letter from Carol and a late Sunday paper. Funny, I've been writing Carol for years but I can't read all her letters. She was fine. She's coming to visit me on the 6th. It's getting kinda cold to be setting up. I don't have but one sweatshirt, and it needs to be washed. I'll be glad when I can get another one. I wrote to Susan to tell her the paper hadn't come in 2 weeks. When she started the paper, I was at Camp J. When I came out for my hour tonight, I stopped by Fred's cell. He was looking pretty bad. He is letting the date he has get next to him. I asked him if he wanted something to read. He said yes, and he will try and read it. I'll be in the same cell in a couple more weeks. Tonight was the first time I feel relaxed on this side. When I looked at Fred tonight, I thought about myself. Being on this side I know for a fact 3 guys want me dead. They can't wait for the 1st of the month. They are counting down for me to die. The guy in Cell 11 just tried to bring Tyrone out there by saying, 'I'll dash you down with something.' I know they are wondering what's going on in my mind because I keep the light on till 4 a.m. and I never say much. The only time I talk to anyone is when they ask me something. I don't hold long conversations with nobody. Writing to Jane Officer is like holding a conversation with her. She could make a very good spokesman. She explains everything. She is the one person I enjoy writing to.

31 January   12.28 a.m. I want to read another book but I think I'll take a nap. Looked out of the window at the rain. Won't be on the yard tomorrow. Read *Phantom Gunman*. It was so-so. 6.10 a.m. I woke an hour before breakfast and for some reason I was afraid. Laid there trying to figure it out. Could be that it's hours before 1 February – or is it because I want to sleep? The thought that if Fred gets executed on the 5th, I'll probably be next. I feel that the worst has come down on me. Jackson and Toothpick brought the food. The 2 hours' nap I took was good. 9.58 a.m. I just woken for dinner. Unseasoned red beans – I had to pass that up. Still have a pain in my neck. The day passed by with no incident. I'm doing my best to put up with this loud TV. Talked to a guy today about a tape player that works like a hearing aid. That way, I'll be able to turn down the noise in here. I guess I'll get used to it if I'm around that long. Diary, it's 6 minutes to midnight. 24 days from now, I might be walking down that hall to the electric chair. From what I'm told, they shave the head about 15 minutes before midnight. I hate to think about that time, but I got to face the fact that my time could be up. It's midnight now. 24 DAYS LEFT.

February 1991

1 February   The beginning that could be my end. I think I'll try to get some rest. I wonder what today is going to bring. The food was hot this morning. Also, I slept like a baby. It's about time I caught up on some rest. Those few days in the Hole took a lot out of me – the 1st couple of days on this side, also. Anyway, Fred was looking more worried last night. I wonder, do I look worried like that? I want to believe that I don't, but I guess it is showing. I remember Dalton Prejean, how he was. It made him sick and he couldn't even eat regular food. He couldn't even stand to be on the hall for an hour. What kept him going was that he had met a girl named Jennifer while he was going to the Pardon Board. She had seen him on the news and started writing to him just long enough for her to visit him a few times. She spent most of the last seven days he had coming to visit him. Diary, he lived a hard life from the time he got the date. He was next door to me and I know. Okay, diary, Jackson just brought the food and it's kinda cold in here. I wish I could go on the yard. I been locked in for six straight days, but I have been running for a half hour on the hall. Okay, I'll get back to you. Back again and it's 8.05 p.m. and just finished my hour on the hall. Didn't talk with anyone. I did speak to the guy on the other side, Hakim. Like I can see it in their eyes that they don't like it one bit that I be running up and down the halls, but that's okay. I'm not going to let my body down because somebody don't like it. I'm getting restless as it hurt a lot to be so close and yet so far from people that have tried to hurt me. All four of them is in a row too. Each day they come out, they ask me if I want some hot or cold water. Diary, I'm trying to keep myself together. It's just so hard.

3 February 1991

Hello Jane,

Your letter of 21 January arrived, Friday and as always, glad to hear from you and to know that all is well for you and your family. I haven't been doing anything. I did get to go on the yard yesterday and I'm suppose to go today.

Anyway, there is a work line here. They grow all kind of things here. They have cows, hogs, horses, cotton too. They even have a milk dairy. It's very few things that they don't have here. They have camps everywhere around here. They even got football, basketball, boxing and volley ball teams here. It's only the people in population that get to go to the games. Oh, and they got a radio station. It's very nice to know that you and your friends are trying the best that you all can to get rid of the death penalty. I hope that a lot more people like you all would get into it.

The war is all they been talking about on the news. It's hard to believe that the war really started. My spiritual advisor's son is over there. I ask her, did she agree with the Bush decision and she said yes. Sometimes I wonder about her.

Also, I received the books. Thank you again for them. I wrote to you last week about the package that they sent back, and Jane, hopefully you are getting all of my letters. I keep a record of all the letters I write you. I made it a fact that I write to you every week. Your letters keep me going around here. If you only knew how hard it was for me to be in the hold knowing that your letter would arrive and I wouldn't be able to get it. Anyway, your letters usually get to me in five days time – it was one day over due.

Since the war started, I had the feeling that it was going to slow down some. They had talk about the planes on the news – how they was cutting back, but it's not going to last too long.

Anyway, things is looking pretty bad for Kirkpatrick. His date is for the 5th and he still haven't heard any thing. He is looking very worried at this time too. I know what he is going through. I have been there a few times myself, and the way it looks, I'll be there again this month. Jane, I hate it when it get like this. I just don't know what to say to people coming in and out, looking at you. I think they know that they be gettin on my nerve. Anyway, like I'm going to keep my head together.

I'm enclosing the copy of the electric chair ruling. It was a blow. Also, I have been talking to some family member. I also gotten a letter from one of my sisters, Friday. Even my eight year old niece wrote me. She don't remember me but I use to be her baby sitter. I had just gotten out of jail and I was doing bad at the time, I also was trying to stay out of trouble, when my sister run into me and ask me to come stay and keep the baby for her. I also was a sitter for my nephew – he don't remember either.

Jane, I wish that I could set down and talk to you. I'd like to just let you in on all the things that I have done. You might even think that I was a lil crazy. Jane, that's why I don't hold anything against anyone. The only person that I had something against was that police that jump my step brother. He had him handcuff to a chair and beat him with a bat. They beat him until they had him saying what they wanted him to say. They put it on tape so when he went to court they made him look like a fool. Jane, some of my family think that I don't like them because of that. You see, what they did to him, got me here. We were together up until 1.30 a.m. that night. I left him with his friends. What he said was that my brother is capable of doing anything. That got him to the point where he was saying anything. I told him he didn't have to feel guilty about what he said. I know what he went through that night when they had him. He was in his thirties. He had never been arrested before, and they told him that they were going to put some arm robberies on him if he didn't start acting right. When I went to court, the DA kept saying his brother said this and he said that.

It's funny how a man could be lock up for just a statement from a man that was frighten into saying something. Jane, the police who did that to my brother, he got his issue a year or so later. He is doing a life sentence. A couple of years ago, my lawyers was going to talk to him and ask him, would he testify on my behalf on how he had gotten the statement from my brother, but I had gotten a stay. I'm going to bring that up to these lawyers that I have now.

Anyway, I do think of you when I'm lonely. Like I said Jane, your letters have been keeping me going. I put your picture right beside my mother's.

I hope I'll be able to send you a better picture of me this month. Thanks again for the books and I'll have you a letter in the mail, Tuesday.

For now, I'm going to just set here and hope for the best to come. Say hello to everyone, and you take real good care of yourself. Thank you so much for being my friend. Doing time is much better with the thought of you.

Peace
Love/Friendship
Andrew Lee

6 February   12.23 a.m. I didn't get any mail but I did a lil more writing. I'm sitting here feeling cold. Hopefully, I'll get my sweatsuit soon. 6.29 a.m. I hated waking up this morning. It's getting closer and closer to my date. 19 days left, and on the 18th they are going to move me to the holding cell. I think that's when it's really going to get rough. Since this month started out, I haven't had enough sleep to make two days with. 8.30 a.m. This morning, Carol came to visit. She wanted to know all about my feelings and how I'm getting along. She said she'd been talking to my sister and trying to get them together on how serious this date is, which they know already. I'm going to try and call them over the weekend. It's been 3 days since I heard from Jane. Also, I didn't get to go on the yard as the rain been stopping me from going out. I run for half an hour on the hall and in my cell. I've lost a few pounds. I did a lil writing and did a couple hours' sleep. It's been 4 days since I read a novel. It's just I feel so restless.

7 February   12.13 a.m. The night ended with nothing. I didn't watch TV. I read my *True Story* for a while. 6.30 a.m. Good morning diary. I woke at 6.02 a.m. to French toast, and it's very, very cold and I don't have anything long-sleeved to put on. The freeman stopped by my cell like he wanted to talk to me. What he was doing was just checking on whether I'm going to hurt myself because I have this date.

7 February 1991

Hello Jane,

Hopefully at this time, all is well for you and your family, and that you are enjoying yourself. I been waiting for the last four days for a letter from you. Have you been getting my letters?

I heard again on the news that they are still cutting back on the planes to other countries.

Anyway, like Kirkpatrick, who had the date for the 6th, he got a stay during the Pardon Board hearing. They recommend life for him but he had gotten the stay first. How they are going to rule on that, I don't know.

As for me, they are getting ready for my hearing. And Jane, for the last few days, I haven't been able to sleep. The closer I get to that time, the more my nerves act up on me. I have lost a few pounds. I have to force myself to eat. Jane, as you know, I have had seven dates before but this one is dealing with me. I feel my nerves jumping, and the rain have been coming down stopping me from going on the yard. Jane, I feel like these walls is closing me in. These people with these loud TVs have just about drove me crazy. I wish I was over there where you are.

Did you get the package back? It should have gotten there before my last letter. Also, they have set a date on another guy. From the way they are setting all these dates they are trying to make up from last year.

Jane, I'm very nervous. I can't even think right to say what I want to say to you in this letter. Oh, they are going to move me in to the holding cell pretty soon. Jane, right now my nerves is getting the best of me. I'll write to you again soon. Okay, you take it easy and I'm waiting to hear from you.

Love
Peace/Friendship
Andrew Lee

10 February   I ended up the night with a lil TV, a lil reading and before I knew it, it was breakfast time. After I cleaned my cell at 6.20 a.m., I went to sleep and woke up at 10.05 a.m. to eat dinner. I'm still sleepy and I have a letter to write and I want to be wide awake to do it, so I'm going to try for a nap. 11.17 p.m. I talked to my sister Terry. She told me how my mother is worrying herself to death about my sister. I hate to get in touch with them – I have enough on my mind as it is, and right now my heart is so full of sadness I can't even think right. I had to call my mother and she was just crying on the phone and she almost had me doing it. Sometimes, I wish I could let out a few tears. I'm truly sad and I feel like a lost cause. I don't know how I'm going to make it through the night. Don't worry, diary, I won't be a coward and commit suicide because I'm all the way down and out. I feel too bad to answer Jane's letter. Also, I wish they would get it straight with themselves and tell my mother the truth. She is lost on how the Pardon Board works. Also, diary, my mother is hurting because she can't get anyone to bring her here to see me. I definitely would love to see her. I can't remember when I last saw her in person. I'm going to let this sad spell pass over me.

11 February   12.41 a.m. Eight days before I'm moved to the holding cell. 7.46 a.m. I was woken from a dream. I was free and helping some people to move – from where, I don't know. 9.05 a.m. I had yard call and I run for half an hour. Talked with Bob a lil while. Didn't get any mail but I did get the newspaper and tried again to call Jane, but nothing happened. I'm going to get some rest so I can write to Jane. Tried to write tonight, but the TV was too loud and I'm trying to hold my cool for a while longer. I heard a guy say, 'Don't worry about your surroundings. Worry about what you are and who you are. Worry about getting out. No man likes to spend his whole life away from his family.' You know, diary, he was right. The guy who was talking knew it too. Anyway, I'm not letting too much get me down.

12 February   Getting a lil bit closer. An old lighter I had I found a good use for it. A guy named Eaton, he needed one and didn't have any money to get one with. Between 3 a.m. and 4 a.m. I fell asleep and slept hard. They brought breakfast at 6.40 a.m. My nerves have calm down and I feel like my old self again. I needed the fresh air and I have accept the fact that I could have only a few days to live and I'm going to enjoy them as much as I can like I am doing with my enemies. They can't figure me out. One day I'm hard, next day I smile. I never stay in the same mood and they don't know if I have forgive or forgotten. Anyway, diary, you and I have had some good times. I'm just glad that I have been able to talk to you about my feelings when we started this year. I didn't think I would have any happy days, but I was wrong. A man must enjoy while he can. It's 7.22 a.m. and they just brought the jumpsuit for yard call. It was very cold outside, but I needed the fresh air. It was good, and I ran for a good 45 minutes. My mind was somewhere else. I thought I was on my way home. I wrote Jane a letter. She is going to write a letter to the Board if she can't make it. 7.58 a.m. It is very cold in here. I want to watch a lil TV but I don't feel like setting up to do so.

12 February 1991

Hello Jane,

Both of your letters arrived, Friday. I didn't answer them back because I thought maybe that I was going to get in touch with my lawyer, Monday. Also, I had been feeling kinder down and out. I don't know what is happening to me, but I have been letting lil things get me down. I have tried very hard to forget about what happen to me but each night it get cold, I think about it. Jane, I don't even remember if I told you in my last letter that they had set the Pardon Board hearing for the 22nd. Like, that got me nervous too. Whatever is going to happen is going to be on that day. I been waiting a long time for this but I was also told that some other judge had made a ruling. He don't want the chair used until he make his decision. That could be another set back. Jane, I want some off of Death Row. I want to be where I can write in peace. I can't do it setting here knowing that I could die the next day.

Also, it's another thing – I'm not in the good place. In the past, I have had conflict with four of these guys that I'm on the tier with now. I'm not going to make trouble for them but I don't know what they are going to do. They have ask me if I wanted some water but I never let them get any for me. Even if I was going to try and do something to them it's nothing I could do. I told you that it's a once a year thing that all of us meet without handcuffs on and no one in their right mind is going to mess that up.

And another thing, the hold is not for me. I like writing to you too much for that. Anyway, when your letter arrived, Friday, I tried to call you the next day, and the next. It's no way that you can call me. If you want to talk to me and it's an emergency, you would have to call here and talk to the warden, then he would call over here for me to call you. Like, I should be done talking to you before you get this letter. It definitely would be nice to talk to you. You know Jane, I had wrote and ask you if that was your phone number on the label. You must not have gotten that letter because you never did say anything about it.

Anyway, I talk to my sister, Sunday night. I explain to them how serious it's going to be for the hearing. I also ask again if they got everything set so if things turn for the worse, no way I want my body left here in this place – I want my soul to blow free. So if there is a after life, I won't wake up looking at these bars. Like I told you before Jane, feel free to let your friends read what I write. You and your friends are doing a lot more than a lot of people here in America. If it wasn't for Amnesty International a lot of people wouldn't know how hard it is for a person on Death Row. A lot of executions would take place too.

Jane, I'm very much happy to have you on my side. I'll be mailing off my diary from the 1st of this year to you, on the 22nd. I want to add the mood that came over me while I was there – at the Pardon Board.

You know Jane, I feel very good and a lil funny. What I am

going to send to you is all my moods, feeling and thought toward this execution date. You'd be surprise how a person can change knowing that he could die on a certain day. Right now, I have it on my mind.

Anyway, I'm sending you this picture of most of the people here on Death Row. Jane, I'm going to write to you tomorrow – and you should be hearing from my lawyer soon. I also found out that the more letters written to the Pardon Board, the better.

Okay, you take it easy and I'll let you know what my lawyer have to say.

Love
Peace/Friendship
Andrew Lee

Sorry for the mistake, but it's cold in here and I don't have any long sleeves. I use my only sweater to go on the yard with.

13 February   12.09 a.m. It's getting very close to that time. This time next week, I'll be up front in the holding cell. That's when things is really going to get rough. All we can do is hope for the best and look for the worst. Just 12 days left and I don't see any way out. I wonder whether my lawyer will come up with something. I'll find out today when I call. 3.24 p.m. I just finish reading Jane Officer's letter and it brought tears to my eyes. She touch my heart. For a long time I been wondering if I could cry. I know now that it is possible for me to do so. Her letter, diary, made me realise that I have hurt my family for too long by staying away from them. They love me just as much as I love them. My emotions, diary, have been touched in a very special way. Right now, my heart is beating very fast. I want to live to be able to say to her that she has brought new meaning into my life. I'll always be beholding to her. I wish I could reach out and put my arms around her. 9.45 p.m. I just talk to Jane Officer on the phone. She sounded funny, like I sounded funny to her. I also wrote to her. I had to send out my chain and cross.

13 February 1991

Hi Jane,

Your letter arrived today and it was very touching. I had tears in my eyes. For a long time, I was wondering if I could ever cry again. Now I know. Jane, you really have brought out the best in me for you have brought out a lot of new meaning to me. I said in one of my other letters to you, I could see a tomorrow now. I could never give up hope for I know that I have a friend in you. Thank you Jane, for coming into my life at this difficult time.

Jane, you are not telling how many miles away from me, but it took you to open my eyes to the hurt that I cause my family. All these years I have been keeping to myself, for I wouldn't let no one get close to me. With you and all your warm thoughts, it brought me back to the time I left home. I left a house full of love for a life that have me here on Death Row.

Looking back Jane, I could have been a better person for I wasn't bad looking. I kept a smile, I was a well liked person. I just didn't care anymore after my father died. I have told them that I was sorry for all the hard times – all the long nights waiting and wondering if I was dead. Jane, I'd give anything to turn back the hands of time, to be able to make up for all the wrong I have done. A lot of nights I have awaken in a cold sweat. Sometimes, I use to get mad for no reason at all. I still remember the looks on people's faces when I use to hold a gun on them. I'd like to say I'm sorry to them.

Jane, my eyes are open because of you. If I should die on the 25th, I won't be the person that lived a long, hard, sad life. It would be a person who learn that life without a meaning, is a life without a future. Thank you again. And that poem you send, it do say a lot. Yes, it make me feel good to have become a part of you, and it would bring great joy to me if I were able to walk with you, set with you – just do anything with you. I hope that I get the chance to hear your voice tonight. Like, the freeman just came and told me to get ready for the call.

And like in my next letter, I'm going to write down the dates to the letters that I send to you and the ones I got from you. They don't care how many times a person write, so don't feel like you wrote too many – write anytime you feel like it. I'll have another letter in the mail for you as soon as I talk to my lawyer.

Say hello to all your friends for me and you keep yourself well, and thank you again for making me a better person. Until I hear from you, I'll just set here and hope for the best.

Love
Peace/Friendship
Andrew Lee

14 February   1.13 a.m. I just finished doing a lil readiing and I'm going to try and get some rest. 6.09 a.m. Just finished washing and had some breakfast. Did get some rest. I'm setting here on the side of the bed and it's very cold. I'll have to get me some more long sleeves. 10 days left, too close for comfort. 9.56 a.m. I was call out to talk to my lawyer, Nick. He told me he didn't know where he can turn to now because my last lawyer had use all the issues. It look like it's the end of the road for us, diary. He told me he had some friends talking to Josephine (that's Jessica's mother and the grandmother to the dead girl). My nerves is jumping again and they just brought second meal but I pass it up. I lost my appetite. I think I'm going to go without my running my 2 miles tonight and call my family. I need to talk to somebody. I'm just going to lay down and let this bad spell pass me by.

18 February   9.20 a.m. and they just move me to the holding cell. That's the next step to count. I'm setting here counting down day by day to a day I might die on. They are not going to let me go on the yard. Then there's the ones wishing that I die. 10.20 a.m. and I've just been told I have a lawyer callout. 1.50 p.m. Michelle Fournet just call and told me she was on her way up here but she got a call saying that the Governor had given me a ten-day reprieve. That mean that they can't set another date on me till late March or early April. I feel good, in a way, about it. But I wanted to get things over with. I wanted to know if I was going to go or get off Death Row.

19 February   12.05 a.m. I waited all afternoon and night for the answer to the stay that I supposed to be done got. Like, I'm still in the holding cell and I don't feel bad or anything. I just like to know for sure. 6.02 a.m. Just brought breakfast. I had a hard time going to sleep. I had a headache – from what I don't know. Maybe one day I might find out why I have so many. I hope today be better than yesterday. 9.40 a.m. Just finished talking with my lawyer, so I won't be getting a date till after 40 days. Now I can put my mind at rest for a while. I still haven't talked to my mother or sisters and I'll try and call them tonight. 3.17 p.m. I didn't get any mail today. They just came and told me to get my stuff together. They're moving me out of this holding cell. I hoped I'd get a chance to talk to the captain, like I want to leave this side. Hi, diary, it's 7.03 p.m. and I just finished getting my cell together and I also finished doing my hour on the hall. I called my mother. She was fine. Carol, she should come up and see me tomorrow. Oh! I also talk to my brother, the one that have me here. Like, I didn't know what to say and he didn't know. It's been like that for a long time. I guess one day it might change, but for now that's the way it stands. 9.55 p.m. Wrote to Jane. I wanted to let some of the other people know who was concerned about me, but I didn't have the stamps to do so. I will get around to letting them know.

19 February 1991

Hello Jane,

Your letters of 7, 9, 11 and 15, all arrived at the same time, yesterday. It's funny how they held them so long. I was reading them when I got the call from Michelle, saying that the Governor had given me a ten day reprieve. That mean that my date will be reset in about two more months, but it also could be reset in a few days. I heard on the news today, that the Governor was going to be out of town for the 25th, and that's why he gave me the ten days, but my lawyer had something different to say. I'll let you know what ever come up.

Anyway, thank you again for being my friend. Jane, each time that I hear from you, it really make my day a better one. Hopefully, I'll be around to meet you someday. In one of your letters you said that you would come over to visit me (that would be nice) but you will have to be on my visiting list. Send me your date of birth and I could have your name added to my list.

Somehow when I went to the hold, a lot of your letters got misplaced. I was in the hold when they went through my stuff. They even threw away my paper clips.

Anyway, how are you at this time? Hopefully, all is well and that you are not letting the cold get next to you. Yes, I do wish that I could be over there. I would love to play in the snow and I wouldn't mind removing it out of your drive way.

I'm going to write again. They just came and told me to get my stuff together, they are moving me out of the holding cell. Okay Jane, like you take real good care of yourself and family, and say hello for me.

Peace
Love/Friendship
Andrew Lee

20 February   12 a.m. Well, diary, I can rest tonight. We won't be going on the yard tomorrow with all this rain coming down. You know, diary, I feel a lot different since I got the stay. You know we were nervous about the whole thing, but we are still in hot water. These 40 days is going to go by fast just like the ones just past. 6.19 a.m. Eaten breakfast. Didn't try to sleep till 4 a.m. I was thinking about my friend Jane and wondering if my lawyer had call to let her know that I had gotten a stay. They were too busy for me to call her last night. Hopefully, I'll be able to do so soon. The letter I wrote won't get to her until Sunday or Monday, and that's the date I had. 8.56 p.m. Diary,

I just woke up from a 3 hour sleep. I couldn't believe it. It been so long since I slept that long. I also had a dream that Tyrone and I were friends. Also, I slept with my head on the bars – that's something I don't do. Right now I'm still sleepy and very hungry. I ran out of food Monday. I'm going to take some multiple vitamin pills to help me through the night. I got about 8 or 9 hours before breakfast.

25 February   12.11 a.m. You know, diary, if I wouldn't have gotten the stay it was a possible chance I would have been dead by now. I wonder, diary, when it's all going to be over with. Sometimes I wish that I would wake up and find that this was all a dream. I miss the outside so much until I have gotten so that I hate to look at TV. I need to see the world or be taken out of it. I'm tired of being the walking dead.

26 February   12.23 a.m. Just think, diary, I could have been dead now. Somebody was looking down on me. 1.28 a.m. and just finished doing a lil reading and I'm going in for the night, and hopefully I'll be able to sleep. 6.28 a.m. Just finished eating breakfast and I did get some rest. I woke up feeling good, but now I feel bad for some reason. I'm wondering where I'm going to get the money to send out the rest of these books. 11.11 a.m. I been standing up for an hour trying to get out some of the stiffness from yesterday. I don't think there will be yard call, so it will be some time tomorrow before I'm out for my shower hour. 1.50 p.m. They just brought mail. I got a letter from Jane that was 26 days old. I also got the Sunday paper that should have come yesterday. These people hold mail like they're mad with Death Row people. Nothing went on today or tonight. I'm still waiting for my shower hour and I'll be out at 1.30 a.m.

27 February   I got the feeling that, later on today, I'm going to get a call saying that another date has been set on me. 1.30 a.m. I came out for shower and ran 50 laps. I didn't turn in till 4 a.m. I need some rest now, so, hopefully, they won't call me too early for the yard. 6 a.m. Just finished eating breakfast. 8.50 a.m. I was just awoken for yard call from a dream. I was in a dream where I was falsely accused of killing a man. I was on Death Row. I tried to get help but no-one would help me. A whole lot of women came marching down the street – for what I don't know – but, diary, everything was real. I got to get out of here. This time is driving me crazy. 10.41 a.m. Just finished eating. I ran 58 minutes on the yard.

27 February 1991

Hello Jane,

It is 12.36 a.m. I just wanted to drop you a few lines to let you know that the diary I sent to you is on the way. I held back from writing over the weekend because I didn't have but four stamps left, and I wasn't sure if I had enough on the diary I sent. After it didn't come back Monday or Tuesday, I figure then that it was on the way.

Anyway, I been feeling much better these last few days. My nerves was getting next to me. Right now I'm thinking if they are going to reset the date today. If they do, I'll have one for the 27th of next month.

It was definitely nice to hear your voice. Sorry, that I felt nervous, but all these people setting there made me so. Also, I was glad to hear that all was well for you and your family – and I'm also keeping another diary for you. I guess you had to laugh at some of the stuff that I wrote. I was so messed up from having the date. When I read some of the stuff, I didn't even remember writing it. You know Jane, it would be nice to set down one day and read it with you.

Anyway, the war is just about coming to an end. I'm glad of that – too many have die already.

Thank you for being my friend, and I'll always be your friend. So, you take it easy, and say hello to all.

Peace
Love/Friendship
Andrew Lee

March 1991

1 March 12.23 a.m. I'm going to do a lil writing, then turn in. I already had my 3 days' yard call for this week, so I didn't have to get up early. 6.30 a.m. and just finish eating breakfast. I woke up with my leg sore and so I have my mother and family on my mind. Hi, diary, it's 10.20 a.m. and they just brought 2nd meal. I thought something was wrong. No-one woke me up for the broom and mop, but the guy said he did. I guess I was real tired. 3.04 p.m. Just finish eating 3rd meal. No mail today. That's a bad way to start out a new month. 7.50 p.m. I didn't run my 2 miles on the hall, but I did run in place in my cell for a lil over an hour. I didn't even stay on the hall for the hour.

3 March 1.19 a.m. Nothing happen tonight. 6.30 a.m. Eat breakfast – just. I woke up feeling very lonely. I need some out of this place. My body is beginning to feel this emptiness. Each morning is getting to be a lil harder to face this life. It's been times when I've forgotten to talk to you, diary. I wonder if I'll be able to do anything free again? I wonder if I'll be able to just shout free words? Diary, I'm hurting this morning. I wish a family member would just come up today. 10.25 a.m. Just finish eating 2nd meal. It was cooked, for a change. I have Michelle Fournet's home phone number. I'll try to call today. 3.05 p.m. and just finish eating 3rd meal. 6.12 p.m. Had my hour on the hall and talked to Michelle Fournet about my whole family. Everyone was well.

4 March 1991

Hi Jane,

Thanks for the card, and it was definitely nice to hear from you. You should have gotten the diary by now. Also, I had wrote you a letter a few days ago. How are you at this time? Hopefully, all is very well.

I hope that you were able to read most of the stuff. Some of it didn't even make sense to me. You know Jane, I went over some of my past diary. I couldn't believe some of the stuff I had wrote while I had a date. Jane, I know now for a fact that a man lose his mind when he have a date. Hopefully, you didn't laugh at me.

For the next few days, I'm going to read everything that I have wrote. I want to get to know myself through the hardship that I have had since I been here. I have been more lonely than I thought I was. Jane, it's funny how I have been here so long without losing my mind. I guess that's why I have so many headaches. Life is so hard here.

This rain stop long enough for me to go on the yard. It felt good to be out there. I still haven't gotten use to being on this tier. The people on this side let their self go too much for me. I'm going to try for a move when everything is worked out about this next date. I had called my lawyer. The date will be reset for sometime next month. I'm not letting it get me down.

I had talked to my family, or should I say, they talked to me. I didn't get in twenty words. They did say that all was well.

What have you been up to? Have you been running around the countryside again making me jealous of you? You know, you bring a smile to my face when I hear from you. I would like to be on one of those small islands too, or catch one of them trains to anywhere. You know Jane, if I was free at this moment, I'd run up and down the street hollering that I'm free. I wouldn't care how cold it was. They wouldn't even have to give me a ride – I'll walk! Jane, if you only knew how bad I want my freedom.

I'm glad that the war is over. They haven't added up on how many is dead. It's no telling what the count is going to be. Hopefully they will have peace for a long time to come.

Okay, I'll be writing to you again soon. Thanks again for being my friend. You really play a big part in my life.

Love
Peace/Friendship
Andrew Lee

6 March 1997

Hello Jane,

Your letters of 24 and 28 February arrived today, and as always, glad to hear from you. How are you at this time? Hopefully, you and your family are enjoying all those wonderful things that life has to offer over there.

Let me say this – like the store you bought the headset from, they didn't put a return address on the box. The rule here is that they must have one. They had the package sent to the dead letter and package office. Then, it's going to be placed in the dead parcel, whatever that is. I wrote to the post-office to see how they can have it sent to you, but I haven't received an answer. I'm enclosing this reason why. You might have to get the store to write to the Angola post-office. I never had this happen before, so I don't know what to do at this time.

I was wondering if you had gotten the diary? I have my copy too so if it would have gotten misplace, I could have replace it. Jane, I felt good sending you that copy. From the first time that you wrote to me, I knew that you were a special person. I'm very much happy that you started corresponding to me. I feel as though I knew you before. With your help, this time haven't been so hard for me. Your letters make a bad day into a good one. I'm glad that you share all your adventures with me. I definitely hope that I could come to your country one day. I would love for you to show me around.

I didn't get the money order. I'll let you know when I do. The mail here have been kinder slow. All your letters been coming on the same day. Yes, I was surprise to get four letters at one time.

Hopefully, you read over my diary first before you read it to anyone else. I said in my last letter, I couldn't believe what I had wrote. Jane, you could share it with Jan if you want to. It would give him a good idea what a date can do to a man. You know Jane, the closer I got to the 25th, the darker my world was getting, and at this time, I feel kinder shame. I don't know how you are going to look at me now after I told you that I didn't let this date get me down. Anyway, don't hold it against me, Death Row is a hard place to live on.

I can't wait to get your next letter. I definitely want to know how it was for you to read something that came from a man that was on his last days. And Jane, this is a time in my life where I need a friend. My next date could be my last – and don't thank me for entrusting you with the diary, I wanted you to have it. I had already told my sister that if things turned for the worse that copy was to be sent you. I wouldn't have had it no other way.

Anyway, I didn't get to go on the yard today, and it's my time to come out for my hour on the hall.

You say hello to Chris and all your family for me, and I'll await to hear from you. Hopefully, I'll have things worked out about the headset. What I want you to do, is hold this copy. If the headset don't get to you in the next few days, send it back to me, okay?

Love
Peace/Friendship
Andrew Lee

7 March   1.45 a.m. I'm doing a lil writing for a guy who can't write. I won't go in till 3 a.m. Oh! Nothing happen tonight. 6.28 a.m. and they brought breakfast a lil before 6 a.m. I took my time eating it since it was hot for a change. 6.57 a.m. and just been called for yard. 8.49 a.m. I came off the yard at 8.02 a.m., showered, changed my bedsheets, and now I'm going to try for a nap. 3.12 p.m. I took a nap but I definitely don't feel as if I did. I feel so restless. Didn't get any mail. I've been running low on stamps and a lot of other things. I owe a guy 10 bags of chips for the newspapers that he's been sending me.

11 March 1991

Hello Jane,

Your letters of 4 and 6 March arrived today, Monday, and as always, glad to hear from you. How are you and everyone at this time? Hopefully, life is being kind to you all. The letter that I wrote you last week, it came back so you should get it along with this one.

I hope that you understood most of my writing. As you can tell, I don't write too good. I forgot to tell you that I'm left-handed, and I write up side down most of the time.

Anyway, on the 7th, they had an article in the newspaper about the electric chair. It said that when they made out the Bill for lethal injection, they fix it so that they can change our sentence over it. I tried to call my lawyer to find out more about it but he wasn't in. I do know that they are going to file a motion on it. I'm getting kinder nervous. When I talk to my sister a few days ago, the Pardon Board lawyer that I have, called again.

Jane, I definitely feel that my time is running out. The last few days, nothing seem to be looking right. I tried to picture myself being around for the summer but I can't. Jane, I don't know what to say about myself at this time. I guess it could be from being on this tier. These people don't think that the death penalty is serious. Most of them wasn't around in 1987 when all them people got executed. The same thing could come up again. They are trying now to cut down on the appeals. If they do pass the Bill, a lot of people is going to go real quick.

I talked to the guy in the next cell from me. He said that if he could ever get out of watching TV so much, he could write a book. I laughed at him. Jane, that guy is over forty years old and don't even go outside because he think he is going to miss something on the TV. I'm going to try and make a move real soon. I want to be around people that understand that every day is a joyful one to be alive. I could go at anytime. I don't want to go thinking that I didn't try to help myself.

Anyway, my mother never did get up to see me. She can't get anyone to bring her. I feel bad at times because I don't really know what she look like these days. I remember her from the last time that I saw her.

You know, now that I think about it, my sister that got killed, I could have pass right by her and wouldn't have known who she was. Jane, I wish that I could turn back time. I guess that's why I can't sleep too much. It's many nights I have lain up here wishing that I would see a family member. I told my sister I don't have a life time to wait to see any one of them. Jane, the times that I talked to them, they had to tell me who they was. Right now, I feel very hurt inside. I don't like to let them cross my mind, it's a pain.

Anyway, it's funny that you don't know about grits. It's some kind of grain. It taste good when it's cook but that's not too often around here. Also, the routine around here is changed all the time. Nothing is the same for very long. I don't mind the way they bring the food – it's the way the shower hour run. It might be thirty to forty hours before a person come out. When a person come out first, he don't even need to think about coming out the next day. It's like that with the yard most of the time. Sometime eight or nine days might pass before I could get outside. If it rain for a minute or two, that's it. During the summer time, I'll be lucky to get outside for the weekend.

It's always something coming out in the newspaper here. What I'm going to do is just start cutting out some things that I think you might like to have. Also, I never did get the money order – it must have gotten lost in the mail. Oh, and thanks for the LIFE LINE. The *Wing of Friendship* is a nice name. It's good to have a friend so far away. The letters you all be writing really help.

Okay, Jane, you say hello for me and I'm going to put you another letter in the mail in a couple of days. I should be done talking to my lawyer by then. And I put in your name today for my visiting list. Like, you should have some paper sent to you in about two or more weeks. Okay, you keep yourself well.

Love
Peace/Friendship
Andrew Lee

12 March   6.44 a.m. Last night, I doze off for a while. I must have been really asleep to miss from talking with you, diary. I finish taking a shower and had a doctor callout. I'm waiting to go and see him right now. I hear them coming with the chains right now. 7.02 a.m. and just come back. Like, they want me back at 7.30 a.m. I'll explain everything when I finish taking all the tests. It's suppose to take 5 hours. 9.11 a.m. Just come back to go down again in an hour. They draw blood 5 times. I had to pee 5 times and I still have to go through more tests. 9.15 a.m. Just come back from another test and did the same things. 11.14 a.m. Another test, and another to go. Also, I just saw Debra and Sarah (Ottinger). They are waiting to see me after the doctor finish. 12.20 p.m. and just finished taking the last blood test. They are going to let me know the result: when, I don't know. I got 4 stamps from Tony James. As of now, I owe 4 different people stamps.

18 March 1991

Hello Jane,

At this time, I still haven't found out for sure if I have a date. I ask the Classification Officer to call this morning to check. He came back and said that I don't have one. What got me is that my lawyer said that I have the Pardon Board hearing for the 5th of next month. Since I been here I never knew anyone to go before the board without a date. Somebody is playing tricks on me. I'm going to try and get in touch with Michelle

Fournet, she is the one that is going to represent me at the Pardon Board hearing. She should know for sure if I have one.

Anyway, your letter of 10 March arrived today, Monday. I was setting down getting ready to write to you when it came. The money order came, Friday. Thank you again for sending it. I'm going to send and get me a sweatsuit and some socks. The socks that they give out here, they wear out real fast.

I was glad to hear that all is well for you and your family. Also, I wish that I would have known that it was Mother's Day over there, like I would have made you a card. Like Mother's Day in the USA is on 12 May.

Jane, I'm definitely sorry that they don't let Death Row make anything. I'm very good at making things out of paper. I'm going to ask one of the guys on high security if they could mail out something made out of paper. Jane, I could make boxes that you would have a hard time believing that it was made out of a book. I will let you know in my next letter if I could get someone to mail it off for me. I'm going to start working on it anyway. I might just get lucky and find someone.

A lot of time I feel guilty just setting here doing nothing when I could be doing something that you could use for your house. I use to make them to sell. If it wasn't for a guy name Lawrence, I still would have been making them. Him and a guy name Jimmy had gotten into it and he told the freeman that Jimmy had gotten me to make him a jewelry box with the escape plan inside. Both of them is dead now. Jimmy got executed in 1987 and Lawrence got executed in 1988. Since then, they don't let nothing go out but drawing, and I definitely can't draw.

Anyway, on the 15th of this month, they turn down Tony James' case. He is like me. They been trying to execute him. He have had nine dates already. I hate to say this, but he is a couple of steps closer than me. The last date that he had was in 1989, and he was definitely not his self. His nerves was so bad he couldn't eat, and what he did get down, it came back up. Out of all the people that have had close dates, Tony came very close to losing his mind. I could have been that way myself because I read over some of the stuff that I wrote when I had the date in 1989 when I came within hours. I had to laugh. I think maybe that I was a lil off.

Anyway, I talked to my mother over the weekend. She is trying to get away here to see me. Jane, this place is set deep into the woods. We are lost to the outside world. Right now they are working on a store to sell everything. The way it seem, they are just going to take us completely off of the map.

I think that I'm losing some of my hair. I got it cut so that it would grow back even, and it grown back a lil bit too slow for me. I had it cut a month ago and it still look like it haven't grown an inch. I wash it every day, that might be the reason why.

I'm glad that I have you for a friend. I can just forget that I'm here when I think about some of the things that I have learn from you. Anyway, I'm glad that you can get out and enjoy yourself, and it definitely make me feel good to know that you and your family have a very close relationship. It's my fault that I didn't look back when I left home. I'm trying my best to make it up to my mother.

I'm going to try and get in touch with Michelle to find out if I have a date for then. So, until then, you keep yourself and family well. I will set here and wait to hear from you.

Love
Peace/Friendship
Andrew Lee

21 March   12.16 a.m. I'm turning in early. 6 a.m. French toast for breakfast was warm. I feel like something is going to happen this morning. 7.54 a.m. and they just finish shaking me down. I didn't have nothing for them to take. 10.10 a.m. Second meal and the pie was good and I got an hour's rest. 11.30 a.m. The mail came early and I didn't have any. 5.30 p.m. and third meal was red beans. They came back and gave us a cold cut sandwich. I bought some more food from the store. I gave Jackson 2 picture frames and a jewelry box to send to Jane Officer in England.

26 March 1991

Hello Jane,

Your letters of 15 and 19 March arrived yesterday. Like, I want to say that I'm sorry to hear that your mother-in-law had passed away, and that it was definitely a coincidence that she passed away on that day. Hopefully, it wasn't too hard for you and your family. How are you at this time? I do hope that you and all of your family are enjoying life as it come. For myself, I'm fine. I talked to my lawyer, Friday, and all is still the same. The Pardon Board had set a date for a hearing on the 5th of next month. But it's no good because I don't have a date. I'm definitely glad of that. I hope that it didn't shock you too much when I told you that. I was suppose to have one.

Let me say this – the reason why I didn't answer your letter back yesterday is because I put my trust in one of the orderly. I put together one of my rush jobs. I made you a jewelry box and two picture frames. It's okay but it's not made right. I wanted to see how much trust I could put in him. So far, he is giving me the run around. I got it to him Friday along with $7.96 in stamps. Yesterday he told me that he had to get it rewrap. Today, he didn't say anything. It was a chance I had to take. If he beat me, I won't be able to do anything about it. Most of the reason why I did it because I would love for you to have something that I made. Jane, you have helped me so much. In your letter of 19 March you made me feel very warm inside. I thank you very much for caring about me. My whole day be complete when I hear from you. Also, I hope the mail got back on time. I had wrote those letters so that one would come every other day.

The Red Nose day sound very interesting. I haven't acted silly in a long time. Did you wear your red nose? I picture you with the red nose and yellow hair, along with Chris. Have the two of you did anything else together? I still think about your trip on that island. Jane, I wish I could get out of this place. I want to see the country you live in badly.

Oh, did you see the Josephine Baker story? She was from

the USA but she lived in London. It was a pretty good picture. They say a part of it was shot in London but I don't know if it's true or not.

Anyway, do you want me to send your copy of my daily diary by the month or just hold on to it? I think that I will start sending them out as the month end. I'll have your copy in the mail to you on the 1st, okay?

I haven't heard anything about the headset. I wrote to the package room again last week. I guess I'll have to write the post office here again.

And guess what? They have put out a new rule saying that we can't call to our lawyers but once a week. If that rule stand, we won't know nothing about our case. The rule say, if we mail on Monday, we won't be able to call until next Monday. A person with a date, he won't even know if he got a stay or turned down.

Also, I'm glad that you had gotten the radio for me. They put out a rule last week saying that no one will be able to get a radio from the outside world. They are selling them their self now. Jane, they are trying to block us completely from the outside world. Every week they're coming up with something new.

Anyway, from now on, every case that come out in the paper, I'll send it to you. I'll have Perry's case in the mail to you in my next letter. Right now, I'm able to get the papers every day. I made a deal with a guy who get the Baton Rouge newspaper. I asked the fellow on this side to help me pay the guy but no one did, but that's okay.

It's very nice that a lot more people is starting to write to people. It definitely ease the mind of a condemn man. You know, that if a person don't have nothing to keep him busy, he would either stay in trouble here or go crazy. Right now, everyone is being cool. It get like that when the cases start coming up.

Anyway, the buffalo stamps, I thought that I had been put some like that on my letters. Since they change the price of the stamps, I haven't ran across any more good ones.

That drawing you made for the paper is alright. I have seen some cards with a hangman rope, a guy getting executed by the chair, lethal injection. I have seen lots of them with bars but I have never seen anyone against the death penalty with it on a T-shirt. They probably have them, I just haven't seen any.

Okay, I will write to you tomorrow or the next day. I'm going to wait for the answer about the stuff I'm trying to send to you. Also, if it work out let me know how much postage he put on it, and also let me know if all three piece was in the package. Also, I will send that address for the headset to the package room here.

Jane, you take real good care of yourself and family. I hope to hear from you soon.

Love
Peace/Friendship
Andrew Lee

28 March   12.27 a.m. and the guys are talking loudly. It's hard to believe they find so much to talk about after being locked in here so long, especially when they been next door to each other for years. Except for me and a guy who came a year ago, the rest of these people have been in this tier together for 4 or 5 years. Diary, I found out a couple of days ago that the guy in Cell 2, Thomas Ward, he is not letting the guys up front in 1 and 3 and 4 watch the TV. He has made a stick out of ink pens and cardboard so he can reach out and change the TV. They are push button. It's funny how they can put up with all that.

31 March 1991

Hello Jane,

At this time, I'm fine and I'm definitely hoping that all is well for you and your family, and hopefully you all had a wonderful time for the Easter weekend. For me it was just another day.

Everything is still the same on my case. I'm going to have to start calling my lawyer on Friday now. They have came out with a new rule saying that we could only call our lawyer once a week. Like I told you, they are trying their best to cut us out from the outside world.

Also, I still haven't heard anything about the headphones. I guess they're trying to keep them.

Okay, I'm enclosing your copy of my diary. After reading through some of it, I find that I'm a whole different person when I don't have a date. Hopefully, my writing is a lil bit readable for you. Also, I'm glad that it help you to get to know the person that you are writing to. I just hope that one day that I'll be able to set down and talk to you.

Jane, thanks to you, I can see more clearer. I don't have to just set around here all day with nothing to do, I have a lot to think about.

I talked to my mother. l hope one day that I'll be able to see her.

That guy who take the pictures, he haven't been around to retake my pictures. He mess them up when he come a couple of weeks ago.

I should get a letter from you tomorrow. I just wanted to say that I was thinking about you and that I wanted this copy to get to you.

Say hello for me, and you take real good care of your self. Oh, and the article that I wanted to send to you about Perry – like, the paper never made it back to me. I'm going to start cutting out the parts that I want to keep for you.

Love
Peace/Friendship
Andrew Lee

April 1991

1 April 12.10 a.m. I just addressed this diary to Jane, and now I'm going to sleep. And I'm going to stop drinking coffee. 5.57 a.m. and just finish breakfast. I ate the eggs and top of the roll. And I didn't have a problem going to sleep. It would have been the coffee mix I was drinking. 10.14 a.m. and second meal finish. Pork chop. I managed to get an hour or so of rest and I might get a chance to go on the yard today. Hello, diary. It's 2.14 p.m. and I made out on the yard. I ran for 58 minutes.

8 April 1991

Hello Jane,

It was so nice to hear your voice, and to know that all was well for you and your family. I didn't come right in and wrote you a letter. I figure that I was to get a letter from you the next day. Your letters of 27–31 March, and 2 April, all arrived.

Like, I hope by this time, you have received the diary and the package that I sent you. I came in and check my calendar. I put the diary in the mail on the 1st, and the guy brought me a slip for the package on the 2nd.

Before I go any further, I want to thank you again for being so concern about me. I wish that I could get my sisters to feel that way and bring my mother up here to see me. I want very much to see her. When I send in the slip for you, I had my visiting slip change. I took off my brother and sister-in-law and put my younger sister on there. That way I can have someone to ride the bus up here with my mother. I have told her about you.

I would love to work in your garden with you. I told you before, I'm pretty good at farming. I worked in the field a very long time. What are you going to plant this year?

Also, right by the yard, there is a family of wild ducks. It's a mother and seven lil ones. They be watching me as I run around the yard. You know Jane, I feel sorry for them. They are grown up in a prison and don't know that they can fly. The mother just walk around watching over them.

Jane, I wish that I could fly, to just keep on flying until I can't fly no more. I must admit that during the summer time is my hardest time here. It's so much that I could be doing out there, but instead I have to be here, wondering if my name is going to come up for another date. Jane, sometimes I hate to wake up knowing that I'm going to wake up to these bars. I can't even have a good dream any more. Every dream that I have is about prison. I just don't know what to say about that. I guess one day, I will have a better dream.

It came out a couple of weeks ago that the people in California are trying to get them to show execution on TV. I was waiting to get an article on that. I will send it to you.

Anyway, I haven't talked to my lawyer. I was just lying there today waiting to go out and call, but I end up going to sleep.

We went out on the yard at 6.36 a.m. this morning. I was woke for the entire night. Sleep haven't been coming to me lately. Anyway, I told the fellows what you all are trying to do to help us. They said to say hello to you and all of your friends. Anyway Jane, I'm glad that you are my friend. My mind be at ease when I hear from you.

Okay, my dear friend. I'm going to say good night to you. You say hello to your family and friends for me, and in my next letter, I'll be able to tell you if any change have come in my case. So, you take real good care of yourself, and I'll do the same.

Love
Peace/Friendship
Andrew Lee

16 April 12.01 a.m. It feels funny having a letter from Jane and not being able to answer it. Diary, everything is going bad for me this month. I asked Sawyer tonight if he would get the chips instead of the batteries so I can pay the guy with them for the newspapers. I'm still going to be 3 short, like it's 10 bags a week that he wants. I still haven't gotten anyone to help me pay for them, but everybody read them.

22 April 1991

Hello Jane,

Your letter of 13 April arrived, Friday, and your letter of 16 April arrived today, Monday, along with the pretty card. I didn't answer your letter back Sunday night because I'm still out of stamps at this time.

Anyway, around here there are a lot of birds. Muffy will get fat around here. It is nice to see those ducks. I wish that I could set them free. I hate to see them walking around the yard when they can just fly away. I wonder if they are going to realise that they can fly. They are use to being around people – I guess that's why they haven't realise it.

Anyway Jane, I don't dream too often. Being here, I have dream myself out. I can only wish now. This place rob a man of his dreams. I don't even get to hear the latest records on the radio. I don't ask anyone for the use of their headset. I listen at the video during the day time. Anyway, I'm glad that my diary is helping you to understand my life here. Jane, I do appreciate you as my friend – you really keep me going.

Also, thanks again for the help with the sweat pants and socks. I'm putting them up for the winter. It's getting warm down here now. Anyway, the lights is out now and don't want to keep on with this loud typing. I know that I won't be able to get in a nap. I slept today for a while.

Love
Peace/Friendship
Andrew Lee

23 April   12 midnight. I think I'll try for a nap to get myself back on track now that I feel better. I was trying to ring my lawyer today. They had articles in the newspaper about some upcoming death penalty cases and the DA used my name. I know the judge saw it. It won't be so long before I get another date. I'm expecting one. 6.26 a.m. and breakfast was pancakes and bacon, and the cold has come back again bad. The guy in the next cell, he have it bad too. I left my letters to Jane and my lawyer in the bars and woke up and they had gone. Hopefully, the freeman put them in the mail box. 10.32 a.m. and just finish 2nd meal of potato and hamburger. I did get a nap. 4.36 p.m. I did get an hour on the yard. Matter of fact, I ran the whole hour. My watchband has broken and I didn't have it with me, so I ran for the whole hour. I received a letter from Jane that was written on the 11th. The guy named New York sent me another newspaper.

29 April 1991

Hello Jane,

Your letter of 21 April arrived, Friday. I didn't answer it back because of my stamps problem that I'm having at this time.

Anyway, it definitely would be nice to set down and have a long talk with you, and to go and visit some of them places in your part of the world.

You know Jane, the trees here is turn back green. I hope that I'll get a chance to see some flowers or some different trees for a change. I haven't been outside this gate since I went to the hole. It's been even longer since I been to the hospital – where they have flowers.

Jane, I feel very lost being here. I need to set down and talk to someone. I haven't had a constructive conversation in a long time.

My sisters and brothers don't write to me. Except for Welcome, we are the only two people that don't have any family members writing. Don't think that I don't feel bad about that because I do. It hurt a lot when I hear people talking about their families. I never have nothing to say about mine. What I did to them, they're doing to me. I wouldn't know if any of them was dead or alive if I wouldn't read it in the papers. Jane, if I wouldn't have seen it (the news about my sister) I don't think that I would have known about it. I said before, I don't hold anthing against them but I do wish that I would hear from them. It get very lonely to have a family but never hear from them, but I just hope that they don't go back on their word and leave my body here. That would be the worst thing that could happen for me.

The ducks is getting bigger. They are just about ready for a pot. It's another one hanging around now. I hope he let them know that they could fly. I don't know what kind they are but I wish that they could understand me when I tell them to fly away.

I never seen a real fox. I always thought that they were dangerous. Do the foxes just walk around where they want? Definitely let me know about that.

Love
Peace/Friendship
Andrew Lee

30 April Well, diary, this is the last day of this month, and I'm glad. This month was a bad one for me. I'm going to read a Western call *Stranger on the Mojave*. 10.30 a.m. I woke up from a light sleep to write-up for disobedience. I had left some books out before I fell asleep. 2nd meal was beans and rice that I didn't eat. 2.33 p.m. The mailman pass me by – I didn't get any. I need some rest. New York just sent me two newspapers. 7.04 p.m. Woke up from a nap. I had a dream that I was getting out of prison and my two nieces came to get me. They were grown women, and at this time they are only 5 yrs and 7 yrs. Diary, the dream was so real. They were explaining to me who they were and I just sat there listening to them. They were saying I would be living with them, and that I didn't have to worry as they were going to take real good care of me. Diary, I hated to wake up. The one that's five, she looked like my dead grandma on my father's side of the family. Sally, she looked like my sister. Diary, I need some out of here.

May 1991

5 May 1991

Without a Cause

I sit in this lonely cell. I think of all
the lost dreams and hopes that I once had.
I think of what it would be like to be free
once again. I often wonder where did I take
a wrong turn in life. For my life have been
with more downs than ups. No man woman or
child should live the way I have lived. For at times
I never had a purpose. I lived only to encounter
risks. For I always felt to take a risk, I could
learn to be brave. But look at me now ... For my risks and
bravery have me sitting here on Death Row ...

Hello Jane,

Your letter of 28 April arrived, Friday, and as always glad to
hear from you. At this time I do hope that all is well for you
and your family. For myself, I'm well as can be expected. I
just feel kinder down from being locked in for so long.

Jane, you know what I need, is a good home cook meal. I
been eating half cook meals for years. I need something that's
going to make my mouth water. Anyway, the next time that
I get the stamps, I'm going to send you a menu and a store
list. It never change. We have the same thing every week. For
the store list, the prices change. We have beans every day. I
will mark the days when the food don't be cook.

Okay, I haven't talked to my lawyer as of this time. From

what they tell me, if I don't hear from them, that mean that nothing new come up on my case.

Again, I will be sending the diary off to you very soon, so please keep yourself and family well. Also, I hope that all of your trips are safe. I wish I could take one with you but since I can't, you have fun for both of us. Also, smell a flower for me.

Your friend always,
Andrew Lee
Love/Peace to you

7 May 1991

Hello Jane,

Your letter just arrived, along with the card puzzle today, Tuesday. As you know, I was very much glad to hear from you.

Jane, to these people here, they want us dead and forgotten. I know that they are trying to break our spirit but I won't let them break mine. I been learn to do without anything. I had told you that I had been put my radio in my box. As long as I can get out on the yard from time to time, I'll be alright.

Jane, I made a big mistake in letting these people put me on this tier. On this tier, it just don't have no togetherness. It's people on this tier that don't even speak to certain people. When I come out for my hour on the hall, I ask everyone if they want some water. I don't have no picks and choose who I ask. The way I see it, we are all in this boat together. That's the way it was when I was on the other tier.

Jane, my friend, I hope that you don't think bad of me but like I have gotten to the point where I don't want to let any of these people here read my books or papers. I do all the getting, and they do all the reading. A lot of books that I get from the trade-in, I don't read them kind. It's not in me to be selfish, but I can't even get help with the postage – that's why I don't have any stamps now. Jane, it's fifteen people on this tier and twelve of them like to read the papers, and nine like to read books. Then there is the people behind me. Jane, do you think that I'm wrong for feeling that way? No-one give me anything to read. Anyway, I'll wait for your answer on that one.

Jane, I'm telling you this because I want you to know that it's not just getting a date that can drive a man crazy here. It's a lot of other things that go on to put a man on the wrong track. When that guy dashed me down, Jane, I nearly went crazy because I couldn't get next to him. At that time, I was messed up in the head. Jane, I'm a person that get around things. I don't go around starting nothing with no one. I have my hopes on getting off of Death Row. I want some freedom. I want to see a lot more of this world before I go under.

So my friend, until your next letter arrive I'll set here and think about all the wonderful things I could be doing in your part of the world. Say hello to your family and friends for me, and you take real good care of yourself.

Peace and love
Andrew Lee

9 May   It's some time after midnight and I guess I'll turn in. It's raining outside so I know I won't be able to go on the yard as I'm first out in the morning. Between 6 a.m. and 7 a.m. and they just brought French toast and bacon for breakfast. I had a dream last night that I was back in the country that I grew up in. Diary, the fields and the people all look so real. I wish I could had dream that dream for ever. I ran for my half hour on the hall. It's somewhere between 8 a.m. and 9 a.m. 10.11 a.m. Update: I was call out for the hospital. It felt good to take a ride after been locked up for so long. I saw some flowers and some women. The hospital callout was two months overdue. I got another watch. It don't have a band, but it works.

15 May 1991

Hello Jane,

Just a few lines to let you know that another date have been set on me. I was holding back to write you but the letter that I wrote to you, Monday, came back to me because I didn't have enough postage on it.

I was waiting to hear from my lawyer so I could have given you some more information on what's going on. He told me that he was going to have a meeting with Judge Hymel, Tuesday, and that he would call up here to let me know how it turned out. He must not have gotten in to see him because he didn't call. He also told me, that if he didn't call that mean he didn't get back in time to do so.

Also, I asked if he could get you in to see me if the visiting paper keep taking so long. He said that it was possible to do so.

Anyway, my friend, I'm not going to let all this get me down. I have already prepare myself for the worse. I also ask my mother again if she have everything set, so if I do get executed, she have everything in order.

Okay, I will write to you tomorrow night if I hear from my lawyer. So, you take it easy until then. Say hello to everyone for me, and I'm sorry that this letter is late getting to you. Your friend always.

Love
Peace/Friendship
Andrew Lee

19 May 1991

Hello Jane,

First of all, let me say this – the date I had for the 4th have been reset for the 16th or 17th. Like, right now, I'm not sure which day it is on. I tried to call you today at 2.30 p.m., my time, but I couldn't get the line. I found out about the change in the date on Friday. He changed because he didn't let my lawyer know that he had set one. Also, I'm going to call him tomorrow to find out just what day the date is set for.

I also had found out, Friday, that the Pardon Board hearing was set for the 3rd of next month, but now it will be reset.

Anyway, what a coincidence that I was going to have a date on 4 June, the same day that my first letter arrived to you. I was definitely shocked. Also, it don't feel like I have been corresponding to you that long. I guess it's because that I'm locked up and time don't really mean that much to me. Also, I have found a good friend in you. It hurted when they came and shook us down, making us get rid of all of our letters except seven of them. The rule have always been like that but they wasn't doing anything about it until this new warden took over. I still have all of your letters – I had them put in storage, but the only way I could get them is if I get off of Death Row and go somewhere else.

Right now, this place is a modern day slave camp. The field work here is long and hard. At one time, people had to work from can see to can't see. They grow just about everything up here. If a person say that they are not going to work, they get locked up in the Hole.

Okay my friend, I hope that it would stop raining so that I could go on the yard. The weekend was long and loud for me. Right now it's 8.33 p.m. and I can't wait for midnight to come so that they will cut off these loud TVs. Again my friend, take care of yourself.

Love
Peace/Friendship
Andrew Lee

23 May   12.14 a.m. Turning in for the night. Hopefully, tomorrow will be a better one. 6.34 a.m. I forced myself to sleep. I was awful hungry and woke up the same way. For breakfast, French toast and cold cut. I ate some of it. It still hasn't set in about the date, and I still don't know for sure if it's been set. 10.22 a.m. I started out to take a nap, but Eaton came and woke me up to use my hair comb. I didn't get mad or anything. That guy is very off. Like, I'm going to buy him a comb come Saturday. For second meal it was some kinda red gravy. I ate a lil of it. 11.27 a.m. They just brought the store orders. I'm next out on the yard. I have to get me another pair of tennis shoes. I have ran a hole in my old pair. I sent my good ones to be washed, and the hot water drew them up. 12.38 p.m. Just finish talking to my lawyer. I found that my date is for 22 July.

23 May 1991

Hello Jane,

At this time everything is fine for me. I talked to my lawyer today and he told me that an execution date was set on me for 22 July. At first it was suppose to be on the 16th of next month. Anyway like it feel good to know that it isn't too close now.

Your letter of 16 May arrived today and as always, I was glad to hear from you. Also, thanks for the newspaper article. I found it very touching. I had to laugh out at first, then I saw my picture with that big smile on my face. I guess the people was wondering what I was so happy about. Also I liked the way it started off: the moving story of a British widow's correspondence with a man on Death Row. I will have it mailed off to my mother tonight.

Anyway, what have you been up to lately? Hopefully, you are still enjoying all those wonderful things in your part of the world. I kinder put myself in England today when your letter arrived. I was trying to picture the faces of the people reading that article; thoughts of a man without hope – and he have that big smile on his face. You must let me know some of the reaction about that.

Anyway, I wish that I could have been with you at that

concert. I can use some getting away from this place. It getting boring around here. I been reading my western books over and over, trying to pass a day around here. It wouldn't be so bad if I could get some help with some of the readers to get books from time to time. When my books are all read up I don't have any to fall back on when I get bore half to death. You know Jane, a man could lose his mind from not doing anything. My most hardest time here is on Friday and Saturday – that's when the TV is on all night. Ear muffs wouldn't do any good.

Also, the other article that I wanted to send you on how that DA use my name. My lawyer didn't see it and asked me to send it to her so she could make a copy. As soon as I get it back, I will have it in the mail for you. Okay, I'm going to close for now so that I can put this in the box myself. So, you take it easy and say hello to all for me. And thanks again for those little card houses. They look nice setting on my lil table. Again my friend, keep yourself well.

Love
Peace/Friendship
Andrew Lee

31 May   12.00 a.m. Diary, I was just lying here thinking it was time I move to another tier. My hearing is getting bad around here, and right now my head is hurting from the loud TVs. 6.46 a.m. I did get a nap and I didn't eat the breakfast – cream of beef. 10.24 a.m. Second meal finish, and I didn't try for a nap. I got into conversation with Tony and Ford. I'll try for a nap later. 1.37 p.m. Just brought mail and I didn't have any. For the last one and a half hour, I been reading a book by Jake Logan call *Across the Rio Grande*. 4.19 p.m. I don't know what they call that stuff they gave us for third meal. Some kind of ground meat. 9.24 p.m. In from the hall. I run my fifty laps more easy tonight. I'm reading a few more pages of my cowboy book and I will watch a lil TV tonight.

June 1991

3 June   12.01 a.m. Another day has pass me by and I'm still here looking crazy. Hopefully, I'll wake up one day and find I'm not on Death Row. 6.39 a.m. and grits and eggs for breakfast. I did nap and had a funny dream that I had just gotten off a bus and two guys tried to kill me. I took one of them out. I woke up before I got to the other one. Diary, I was looking at the date. At midnight tomorrow, I could have been executed. I hope I hurry up and get this death penalty off me.

4 June 1991

Hello Jane,

It was definitely nice to hear your voice and to know that all is well for you and your family. I received your letter today also. I liked the way you described your trip. Thanks for the postcard. I liked the way those little houses was sitting apart.

Jane, I could come to Britain and find my way around thanks to you. I read your letter over twice. It really made this day better for me.

I was setting here thinking that on this day, I could had been dead. I found myself watching my watch last night when it changed over to the 4th. Jane, it was hard for me not to think of this last date that I had. For some reason, I keep getting the feeling that this is my last, but something always come up in my favour.

Anyway, I call my lawyer yesterday to find out what is going on. I have to take that test over again, Saturday morning. I have to get the right name to that test. I will have you a letter in the mail letting you know the name of it, Sunday night.

Again keep yourself well and I'll await your next letter.

Love
Peace/Friendship
Andrew Lee

13 June 1991

Hello Jane,

Your letter of 8 June just arrived and as always glad to hear from you and to know that all is well. For myself, I'm okay. Today was my first day on the yard since last week. I felt funny out there after being locked in for so long.

Anyway, thanks for the pictures and the card puzzle. Also, I didn't hear from Nick or Sarah today, or yesterday. Hopefully, they will have gotten in touch with you. I told you I didn't mind doing it but as you know, I have to do what my lawyer says. No one was in when I called. I talked to the lady named Barbara, and she said that they didn't say anything to her about it.

And guess what? They got a guy in prison from Death Row in Washington, begging to be executed. He been on the news all week, and they are asking people if executions should be seen on TV. Jane, if I had a way to get to that guy, I would smack him a couple of times. The last guy that pulled that off was a guy name Gary Gilmore. He was the cause that the death penalty came back. He started that in 1975 or 1976. They made a movie about that.

Jane, right now, everytime the news is on, they are talking about the death penalty. I'm definitely sorry that I have a date at this time. If he get his way, a lot of people will die. What he is doing, he is trying to show people that when you get the death sentence, a person might be on Death Row for years. He said that he don't want to wait that long.

Anyway, about the visit. Visiting days is on Wednesday through Sunday. If I still have the date when you come, I will be able to have a contact visit with you. Within seven days of an execution date, a person can get them. Also, you can't bring anything but money with you, and you must have a dress or long pants – no shorts or low cut blouses. Also, about the Pardon Board, they usually hold it the day before the execution date but my date is on a Monday, so they will most likely hold it that Friday, which is the 19th.

Okay, I will have another letter in the mail by Sunday night. So, until then, you take real good care of yourself and family. Say hello to all your friends for me.

Love
Peace/Friendship
Andrew Lee

21 June   12.04 a.m. The days is finally starting to go by fast. I'll be turning in in one hour when the lights go out. 6.30 a.m. For breakfast, cream of beef. I didn't eat it. Also, I had a hard time trying to get a nap, but I finally did. I'm third out this morning. I wish I had yard call so that I could have a little fresh air. 10.15 a.m. Sweat is pouring off of me. I had been running the hall for 33 minutes when they brought the chow wagon. It was fish and potato, but I didn't eat it. I still have some time left to shower after they come pick up the trays. I won't run any more. 11.19 a.m. The cable is out of the TV so I won't be able to watch the news. So I'll start reading *Silverado* again. 1.47 p.m. Just come back from talking with my lawyer. She told me that Jane had called. I didn't get any mail. 3.21 p.m. Hot dogs for third meal. 9.27 p.m. Just been lying around reading for the last couple of hour, waiting on the 12.45 a.m. movie, *Tie me up, tie me down* again.

30 June   12.00 a.m. I'm turning in for the night. I was lying here hoping for a good movie to come on, but none did. 12.19 a.m. Diary, I just happen to roll over and looked out of the window. The moon is full tonight and it's been months since I last seen the moon. 6.28 a.m.

Pancakes for breakfast. I ate them. This is the last day of the month in a few hours. The countdown starts to 22 July. I did get a pretty good nap. I think I'll catch sick call tonight. 12.31 p.m. Just back from taking a picture. 3.04 p.m. Just brought third meal. Some kinda rice. No way in the world would I eat that stuff. I wrote Jane a letter. I still have two and a half hours before I come out for my shower hour. 4.50 p.m. I'm about to read a Western by Tom W. Blackburn. Still an hour and a half to go till shower. Scooter sent my books back and I sent him two more of mine. 7.15 p.m. Just finish talking to my sister. 10.22 p.m. Just finish reading *Patron* and it was a good book. Right now it's close to 4 hours till the lights go out, and 1 hour 26 minutes before July starts.

July 1991

1 July   12.13 a.m. Well, diary, I can start the countdown now. This month is going to be a pretty rough one for me. In twenty-one days from now I could be executed. How do I feel? Funny now that July is here. Anyway, I'm going to do a lot of reading to keep my mind off it. I'm going to try for a nap. I should be one of the first on the yard. 6.28 a.m. Eggs and grits for breakfast. I ate the eggs and biscuits. Also, I did get in a nap. 10.26 a.m. Pork chops for second meal. I didn't eat. Also, I should be next on the yard. It's very hot in here today. The pain is still there in my shoulder. 12.43 p.m. I didn't get but 30 minutes on the yard. I had to stop, it was so hot. Right now, I'm waiting to come out for my shower. This morning, I went for the psychology test. I was out there till 3.25 p.m. I have to visit with the psychologist guy again tomorrow for four or five more hours. Also, I found out that the Pardon Board hearing is for the 19th of this month. Right now I need to take a nap, but I have a five-hundred-question test to answer for tomorrow. The test is out of a booklet called *The Minnesota Multiphasic Personality Inventory* by Starke R. Hathaway PhD and J. Charnley McKinley MD. 8.05 p.m. Just finished taking the test. It took me 2 hours 10 minutes. I need a nap badly now. 8.59 p.m. I will bypass a nap now and watch a movie call *Night Angel*. 10.21 p.m. I should have went to sleep as the movie was awful. It's another one coming on now called *Midnight Seduction*. I'll probably watch it.

6 July   1.15 a.m. The movie wasn't that good. I'm going to turn in now. 6.22 a.m. I did manage to get in a nap, and right now I'm waiting to come out for a shower. I have to meet with that PhD guy again today. 1.07 p.m. Just came back from taking the test. I need a nap. Will try and take one after my hour on the hall. I should be next. Also, I haven't had anything to eat.

7 July   The Governor has made a statement saying that the ruling for the lethal injection didn't apply to me, Tracey and Eaton. I'm the only one that's in danger of being the last person to set in the electric chair. As of now, I have a funny feeling about that. 10.16 a.m. Just brought chicken pot pie. It wasn't any good. 3.24 p.m. Hot dogs and chilli for third meal. I have the clipping on the statement from Governor Roemer. He said that the state had no plans to delay any executions because the chair has been voted out. It didn't start till 15 September. Anyone having a date from now till then stand a good chance of being executed. I did get a nap in.

8 July 1991

Hello Jane,

Your letter of 29 June arrived today, Monday, and as always, glad to hear from you. At this time I'm fine as can be.

I haven't talked to Sarah or Nick in a while. I wanted to call today and ask them if they had read the article that was in the Wednesday paper. From what I hear, he made a statement on Thursday too.

Also, as of now, I'm the only one that is stuck out so far. I'm definitely hoping that I won't be the last one to set in that chair. I got the feeling that they are trying to get one more before they put an end to it.

I can make a lot of things out of paper. There are a lot of people that have something that I made inside of their house. If they wouldn't have stopped me from making things, your home would have plenty of things made by my hands. When all this is over with, I'll put everything together for you. I use to sell the box and two frames 10 dollars. It might seem like a lot of time to set there and put one together, but it's not once you get the hang of it.

Anyway, I'm looking forward to your visit. You should meet everyone when you come down. I think I told you that your visit should be all day since you are from out of the country. It won't be no problem about you getting all your visiting time. Let's just hope that I won't have this date on me.

Have you been getting all of my letters? I wrote nine times last month. You know I was very surprised to see that I did. I knew I had wrote six times but when I saw that I had wrote nine, I realised that the time is passing by very fast for me.

In a few days, they will be moving me into the holding cell. I never did take to that too kindly. I don't like the way that people be looking at me. Everybody have the thought of death on their minds. They are asking me now about this date when everyone know that I have it.

You take real good care of yourself my friend. And again, I'll be looking forward to seeing you.

Love
Peace/Friendship
Andrew Lee

9 July   I talked to Nick, my lawyer. He didn't sound too good about my case. He told me they had located Jessica and she didn't have nothing to add. Neal (Walker) was meeting with Michelle today. They are getting ready for the Pardon Board hearing on the 19th. 3.25 p.m. Franks and spaghetti for third meal. I ate it. 3.27 p.m. I was just called out to my lawyer, Michelle Fournet. She wanted to know if I would submit to be hypnotised. I said yes. 8.56 p.m. I finally finish writing everyone, and my head is hurting. Right now I'm going to rest my eyes.

11 July   12.29 a.m. Almost ten days to go now. This date is coming up too fast. It seem like it's trying to tell me something. Diary, what hope have I this time? If only I could look in the future. I'm turning in for the night. 6.25 a.m. Just finish breakfast. French toast. I ate it. I have a bad pain in my lower back and I feel awful this morning. I had a hard time getting a nap. 10.34 a.m. For second meal, red gravy and spaghetti. I didn't eat it. Right now I'm waiting for a shower. I had an attorney callout. 1.19 p.m. Just back from visiting with my lawyers Nick and Neal. Diary, I feel this is my last go around. I have a bad headache at this time. I let them take my diary with them. The storeman came while I was out there. My nerves is jumping too bad to eat this ice cream.

13 July   12.00 a.m. Been setting here watching a movie that is very boring. I'm turning in for the night. 6.20 a.m. Sweetrolls for breakfast. They wasn't cooked that good. I have that lower back pain again this morning. That mattress is something else. I haven't had a dream in a while. I can't look past the 22nd. I must admit I'm at the end of my rope. 12.08 p.m. At 9.05 a.m. I went to the yard. I had a very bad headache but I did get in a half hour. When I came off the yard I had a callout with Dr Zimmerman. I probably spelt his name wrong, but he came to put me under hypnosis. It worked too. Like, I remember leaving Reginald's house and going over to Donna's house. Then I went to a bar room. I don't know what good it's going to do, but I'm glad that I did remember what I did. Red beans and rice for second meal, and I also made store.

16 July   12.25 a.m. Another day has pass me by. I don't know how I feel about this date. I guess it's time for me to turn in now. I have another callout for today. 6.24 a.m. Pancakes and cold cuts for breakfast. Also I did get a little nap. Right now I'll try for a good one before the lawyers come up here. 10.22 a.m. Second meal just came. I couldn't figure out what it was, so I didn't eat it. The attorney callout is for 11.30 a.m. Right now I'm setting here waiting to come out for a shower. I hate it that I can't go on the yard. If this is going to be my last stand, I definitely don't want to be on this tier, but it's too late now. 4.17 p.m. Just back from visiting with my lawyer. 9.50 a.m. Just back from my hour on the hall. I didn't run but talked to many family members. Also, at this time I'm very hungry.

17 July   12.47 a.m. Another day pass me by and four more days till that time. Also, it has some stuff on the news about me and it wasn't for a stay. Also, I'm turning in for the night. 6.30 a.m. I ate the eggs for breakfast. Also, a nap didn't come easy last night. I'm hoping for one this morning, but I'm sure I won't be able to get one. I should have a lawyer's visit this morning. 10.30 a.m. Second meal, red beans and rice. They were uneatable. 3.44 p.m. Update. I spent about two and a half hours with my lawyer, Michelle, and about an hour with Jane Officer. I had a nice visit with both of them. Third meal was red beans and rice. Right now I'm hungry. 9.52 p.m. Still hungry. I just finish my hour on the hall. I didn't run but 25 laps. Also, I call sister Velma, Carol and Susan. Also, the courts turn me down again today. The Louisiana State Supreme Court turn me down.

18 July 12.01 a.m. Just finish the book and I'm going to turn in now. I have another long day ahead of me. 6.19 a.m. Just awaken for breakfast of French toast. It took me a while to fall asleep. 10.43 a.m. Just came for a visit with Carol. Second meal was chicken. I didn't eat it. Also, I'm very sleepy at this time. Hopefully, I'll be able to turn in early tonight so that I could be fresh for the Pardon Board hearing tomorrow. 1.35 p.m. I been setting here waiting for Jane to arrive, but I guess something must have happened to prevent her from coming. I had a visit with Michelle and made store. I just order ice cream. I wish I could fall asleep for a while. 3.18 p.m. Just returned from visiting with Jane. Had a very nice time. 5.25 p.m. Been clearing out my locker. Macaroni for third meal. 10.43 p.m. I didn't do any exercise tonight. I talked to Byrd, Velma, Susan and Michelle. I dozed for a few minutes, but I don't think I can do so again. It's almost four or five hours till lights out.

19 July 12.16 a.m. Very close to the 22nd. I feel it's the end. Hello, diary, it's 6.40 a.m., the morning of the Pardon Board hearing. I feel kinda funny this morning. Creamed beef for breakfast. I didn't eat it. Anyway, time will tell what it's going to be like. 6.02 p.m. Just came back from the Pardon Board. Two voted for life, the others voted for lethal injection. That mean only one thing – I'm a dead man. How do I feel? Funny. 10.13 p.m. Update. Just wrote Jane and Dee and talked to Nick, Mother, Ronnie and a few more. Also, I'm getting closer to that time. I always wondered what it would be like to know when you are going to die. Now I know. Right now I feel dead inside. Like, I guess people wondered why I laugh so much. That's just to keep me from being sad all of the time. I guess I'll rest for now as I have another long day tomorrow. 11.32 p.m. Wrote Mother.

20 July   12.06 a.m. Time is just about run out now. I just hope it would be less painful for my family and friends. 6.32 a.m. Just awaken for breakfast. I must say I fell asleep without the thought of death on my mind. I have accept the faith. It's not that I want to go, but the decision has been made. Also, it sets me free. 8.41 a.m. Just been talking to Mother and Peterbo. 3.21 p.m. Had a nice visit with Byrd, Jerry, Mother and Peterbo. Right now I need a rest before I come out. 8.21 p.m. I haven't been doing anything but talk on the phone. I talked to Velma and some more people. Also, I got turned down again by the courts. 11.12 p.m. Talked to Barbara, Dalton's friend at this time.

21 July   12.16 a.m. A few hours from now I might be dead. 7.18 a.m. Just finish packing everything up. Waiting to go back to Camp F. Like, I don't feel bad or anything, but it's a funny feeling knowing that in a few hours you could be dead. But I'll be strong to the end. Also, I ate one pancake this morning. I had ate a big sandwich a little before midnight, so I wasn't hungry. Anyway, like, saying goodbye, and always, goodbye. Like, I will make my last walk down the tier hopefully.

19 July 1991*

Jane,

It's 8.47 p.m. I was setting here thinking about you and I wanted to write these few lines to you. I want to thank you very much for all the support that you have given me and I'm sorry that it had to end this way. I felt very uncomfortable setting there saying that I did something that I don't know I did or didn't do. I guess that is the way the world works – and the charge that he brought up from the past, it was dropped on me but they brought it up.

*I received this letter on return to England.

Anyway, I hope that my past wasn't too shocking for you. It was rough but it was a long one.

If I see you tomorrow, you won't know about this letter until it arrive at your house.

What I want you to do is tell everyone that their prayers was really helpful in a lot of ways. I told you before that I didn't have anything against anyone and I will go to my grave that way. I want you to always remember that your support kept me going. I'm not feeling too bad at this time, I just feel bad about all the people that are going to be hurt by my being executed this way.

Jane, my friend, I want to write more but I want to lay down for a while to think about today. Your friend always.

Love
Peace/Friendship
Andrew Lee

The following Death Row prisoners who are mentioned in the text have been executed since 1991, all by lethal injection:
  Robert Sawyer, March 1993
  Thomas Lee Ward, May 1995
  Antonio James, March 1996
  John Brown, April 1997
  Dobie Williams, January 1999.

Afterword

July 1991 was indeed an oppressively hot and humid month in Louisiana. I worked as an attorney at the Loyola Death Penalty Resource Center. We were a small office: three attorneys, an investigator/paralegal and an office administrator. We represented men on Death Row in Louisiana, generally in the final stages of their appeals before executions were to be carried out. I had worked in the office a little over a year and the threat of an execution was always present. We worked around the clock, through the weekends, almost desperately, doing whatever it took to stay executions. The building that housed our offices was an old bank building in downtown New Orleans. It was not air conditioned at weekends, but tended to retain at least some of the coolness of the previous working week through most of the weekend. Sunday nights, however, were unbearable. When I became overwhelmed by the heat, I would take a break from my computer and lie down on the cool marble floor in the hallway outside our offices.

Reading through Andrew's journals and letters this past week, my mind has been flooded with such images and sensations, all characteristic of the two-year period when I worked at the Resource Center. It is both wonderful and painful to read Andrew's descriptions of the men on Death Row and the events that shaped the course of those years. Andrew describes life on Death Row in a way that I suppose I was peripherally aware of, but was unable to appreciate at the time. My own world was filled with developing the factual and legal arguments that would prevail in getting a court or the Pardon Board or the Governor to stay executions. Andrew's letters and journals are treasures because he was so capable of conveying a feeling for life on Death Row.

I did not know Andrew very well until the last week of his life. In the final stages of Andrew's case, Nick Trenticosta, director and attorney at the Resource Center, drafted and filed most of the court pleadings. Neal Walker, the third attorney at the Resource Center, represented Andrew at the Pardon Board hearing along with Michelle Fournet, a private attorney who worked *pro bono* on Andrew's case. I was much more involved in the cases of other men on Death Row, but of course was available to do whatever I could to help the attorneys representing Andrew. In the end, I drafted some court pleadings protesting the fact that the prosecution struck all black jurors from the jury that heard Andrew's case. I met with members of Andrew's family to assist in preparing for the Pardon Board hearing. And, most importantly, it became my job to prepare Andrew for the hearing. This involved discussing with him in detail the crime he was convicted of committing.

I still consider the content of those conversations to be confidential. But what I want to convey is that I spent several hours with Andrew on several consecutive days the week before he was executed, and came to know him well. He shared significant details of his life with me because I asked him to, because it was necessary, because it was the last week of his life. He did so despite the fact that it brought him great pain. Andrew literally believed that he would not survive the telling of some parts of his life. Like many of us, he feared that no one would love him who really knew him. Andrew's courage and honesty moved me a great deal and I felt privileged to come to know him better.

Andrew mentioned his smile in his letters. He had a remarkable smile: a quiet, child-like smile that lit up his face. Yet the sparkle of pleasure was mixed with a hint of immense pain.

Andrew's life, like those of many of my clients on Death Row, was marked by pain and deprivation. He grew up in poverty and enslavement. Like his father before him, he was born and raised on a sugarcane plantation. Andrew was the seventh of fourteen children. The family worked the fields, picking cotton and harvesting cane, and Andrew's father doubled as a chauffeur. Despite the fact that parents and children worked, they were never paid enough to survive. Their lives were bound to the plantation life by credit owed to the plantation store.

When Andrew was seventeen years old, his father became very ill. Initially, a country doctor diagnosed a pulled muscle in his back. Later, when Mr Jones sought competent medical advice, he was diagnosed with cancer of the liver, which by that time had spread to his lungs.

Of all the children, Andrew was most affected by his father's prolonged and painful death. The fabric of his life slowly unravelled.

Shortly after his father's death, when Andrew was eighteen, the family was evicted from the plantation. Andrew found himself thrust from a rural environment into the urban surroundings of Baton Rouge. Not long after moving, Andrew dropped out of school. School records show that Andrew never progressed beyond the second grade in learning. From that time forward, he had been socially promoted to the tenth grade. Testing conducted only after Andrew had been sentenced to death revealed the explanation: Andrew had an IQ of 77.

Not long after moving to Baton Rouge and dropping out of school, Andrew started drinking. He was soon arrested for burgling a convenience store and stealing beer. Despite the fact that he had never been arrested before, the judge denied probation and sentenced Andrew to three years at Angola, where he spent the remainder of his teenage years.

Not surprisingly, Andrew emerged a different person from Angola, one of the harshest prisons in the USA. His youth had been marked by poverty and deprivation, but not by violence. This changed after Andrew's first stint at Angola. He spent the next eight years of his life in and out of the prison, living on the streets while he was free and getting involved in a string of tumultuous and violent relationships with women. He became addicted to drugs and began experiencing psychotic episodes for which he did not receive treatment. Ultimately, he was arrested at the age of twenty-eight for the rape and murder of a thirteen-year-old girl, the daughter of his girlfriend at the time. Andrew was charged with first degree murder, punishable by death.

Because neither Andrew nor his family could afford to hire an attorney, the court appointed an attorney with the Office of the Public Defender in Baton Rouge. Andrew's lawyer had practised law for only four years, which did not qualify him under Louisiana law to represent Andrew at trial. However, another lawyer with more experience enrolled on the case as co-counsel. Even though the second lawyer did not participate actively in Andrew's representation, his enrolment satisfied the state law requirement that Andrew be represented by a lawyer who had practised for at least five years. The trial lawyer's inexperience was ultimately fatal to Andrew.

In Louisiana, a capital trial is divided into two parts. First, a jury of twelve must determine whether a defendant is guilty of first degree murder, guilty of a lesser crime, or not guilty. If and only if the jury determines that a defendant is guilty of first degree murder, the same jury then proceeds to the sentencing phase, in which they determine whether a sentence of life or death should be imposed. If the jury unanimously recommends that a sentence of death be imposed, the court imposes the death sentence. If the jury is unable to reach agreement on the sentence to be imposed or if the jury unanimously recommends a sentence of life imprisonment, the court imposes a sentence of life.

The jury must consider several factors in reaching a determination of the sentence to be imposed. Among those factors that mitigate against imposing a sentence of death, and that are particularly relevant to Andrew's case, are first that the offence was committed while the offender was under the influence of extreme mental or emotional disturbance; and second, that at the time of the offence the capacity of the offender to appreciate the criminality of his conduct or to conform his conduct to the requirements of law was impaired as a result of mental disease or defect or intoxication.

At Andrew's trial there was a legally sufficient amount of evidence linking him to the rape and murder of the thirteen-year-old girl, and the jury unanimously found him guilty of first degree murder.[*] At sentencing, Andrew's inexperienced lawyer argued that Andrew had consumed a great deal of alcohol on the night of the murder and was intoxicated. Andrew's lawyer did not seek funds to hire any experts to evaluate Andrew's level of intoxication and its effect on his actions; nor did he seek any funds for experts to conduct psychological testing and determine whether Andrew had a 'mental disease or defect'.[†]

Such evaluation would have produced a wealth of mitigating evidence for the jury to consider in recommending a sentence in the

---

[*] *The fact that the evidence was legally sufficient does not mean that it really explained the crime. Notably missing from the evidence against Andrew was any explanation of how Andrew, who did not own a car, had travelled a great distance to the little girl's home and transported her to the place where her body was found.*

[†] *The year after Andrew's trial, the United States Supreme Court ruled that all indigent defendants are constitutionally entitled to such funding when they make a showing that it is necessary to their defence. When Andrew's case was tried, there was little funding available for experts and his lawyer did not even request funding.*

case. Years later, in the course of his appeals, Andrew was thoroughly evaluated by a neuropsychiatrist and a psychologist. They concluded that Andrew had experienced psychotic episodes throughout his adult life, that he suffered from organic brain damage, and that he was borderline mentally retarded. Intoxication probably augmented all three conditions when the crime was committed, although it was not clear whether Andrew was experiencing a psychotic episode at that time.

Crucial information regarding Andrew's state of mind when the crime was committed came to our attention only a few months prior to Andrew's execution when we requested Andrew's jail records, which documented his pre-trial incarceration. The records established that two weeks after Andrew's arrest, the jail asked a state psychiatrist to examine him. The doctor diagnosed psychosis and prescribed Thorazine, a powerful anti-psychotic drug. Andrew was told he was taking sleeping pills. The prosecutor never informed Andrew's defence attorney of the psychiatrist's diagnosis, despite the fact that she was under a legal obligation to reveal all information in her possession that was critical to Andrew's defence in the penalty phase of the trial. The state psychiatrist's diagnosis and course of treatment established conclusively that Andrew was psychotic during the period of time when the crime was committed.

The end result was that the all-white jury that sentenced Andrew to death did so without the benefit of crucial evidence mitigating against a sentence of death. Andrew was executed because of his attorney's inexperience, the prosecutor's dereliction of duty, and the criminal 'justice' system's failure at that time to provide a mechanism whereby indigent defendants could secure expert funding.

It would take far more time and space than I have to trace Andrew's progress through his appeals. Suffice to say that the courts never allowed Andrew to supplement the record in his case with the testimony of experts later hired to evaluate him. As a result, Andrew moved through his appeals at a fairly rapid pace. It was not until Andrew had exhausted his appeals and was pursuing a course of successor appeals (the point when Rebecca Hudsmith and Nick Trenticosta began representing him) that the Louisiana Supreme Court finally sent back his case to the trial court for a hearing on the prosecutor's use of peremptory challenges to exclude all blacks from Andrew's jury.

Andrew alleged that the prosecutor had intentionally discriminated against blacks by excluding all potential black jurors from the jury. After a hearing on the issue, the trial court ruled that the prosecutor had enunciated race-neutral reasons for excluding the black jurors. The ruling ignored the obvious bias with which the prosecutor exercised its challenges to exclude all blacks. The appellate courts upheld the trial court's ruling, and the claim of discrimination was turned down for the final time by the United States Supreme Court shortly after 9 p.m. on the night Andrew was executed.

My own participation in Andrew's case, as I have said, was limited. Looking back, I think my most meaningful role was being present with Andrew in the final hours before his execution. It is an impossible task to convey what it is like to spend the last hours of a man's life with him, in prison, watched by guards, waiting for the appointed hour of his death. Nevertheless, it is a task worth undertaking, since Andrew never had a chance to describe what happened.

Several of us sat with Andrew throughout the evening in a large room directly outside the execution chamber. In addition to Andrew and me, Debra Voelker, Neal Walker and Michelle Fournet were there. We sat around a table talking. There were guards in the room as well, but they kept their distance. Andrew was handcuffed and shackled at the waist throughout the evening. His feet were also shackled. We would talk for a while, then Andrew would get up and shuffle away to call his family, and the rest of us would pull ourselves together. We tried as much as possible to take our cues from Andrew. More than anything, he seemed to want distraction and we took turns providing it. Surreal is the only word that comes to mind when I think about that evening. Yet it was real. The state of Louisiana took Andrew's life that night.

One of the most difficult times for Andrew in the long wait came at 9.30 p.m. when we received word that his last appeal had been denied by the United States Supreme Court. Andrew refused to talk to Nick, who called from the office to give him the news, because Nick was crying. Andrew had forbidden any tears.

Andrew came back from the phone to the waiting room and sat down quietly. Then he looked straight into my eyes and asked, 'Why can't they just do it now? How am I going to get through the next few hours?' I had no answer. I tried to imagine that in a few hours his life would be over, but mine would be beginning a new day. I tried to imagine what it was like for him to look at me, knowing this. We stared at each other, and I shook my head. Someone suggested that Andrew purchase something else from the vending machine and we all laughed thankfully. For Andrew, one of the great thrills of the last day of his life was his ability to put coins in a vending machine, punch a button, and receive food or drink. It had been over seven years since he had come into contact with coins or a vending machine.

Forty-five minutes before Andrew was executed, guards removed him from the visiting room, saying he would return soon. Fifteen minutes later, he walked back in with that smile of his, but awkward and blinking ferociously. In preparation for attaching the electrodes, the guards had shaved his head, one leg and, as Andrew pointed out, 'even my eyebrows'. He was embarrassed. He wondered how he looked. Of course there were no mirrors.

Andrew kept blinking. He explained that there were tiny bits of hair from his shaved eyebrows that were getting in his eyes. He was shackled at the waist and couldn't reach his eyes. Neal pulled a handkerchief from his pocket and asked if it would be okay to wipe Andrew's eyes for him. I didn't want to witness this. I didn't want Andrew to be embarrassed, or to worry about how he looked, or to accept help like a child having his nose wiped. He was about to die. Wasn't that enough?

One of the many silences crept over the table where we sat. Andrew laughed. 'At least they let me keep my Air Jordans,' he said. 'I thought they'd take those too, but they didn't. I've spent my whole life running and I want to hit the other side running.' Michelle reminded Andrew that he'd always dreamed a plane would crash at Angola, setting him free. Andrew said it wasn't too late. We all laughed.

The worst moment came when Andrew was led into the execution chamber. It stays with me. Andrew had passed by us in the hall on the way to the door to the chamber. He gave a strained smile and flapped his shackled hands at us. I watched his back after he passed. At the door to the execution chamber, the guards stopped and made Andrew take off his prized running shoes. As he bent to do so, he looked back, directly into my eyes. I will never forget the raw fear in his eyes. There were tears in mine. All pretences were gone.

I spent the next fifteen minutes doing deep-breathing exercises, pacing the floor, looking at the drab prison surroundings, trying to comprehend but not be overwhelmed by the fact that Andrew was being electrocuted in the next room. We were separated by a wall. At some point I decided that action, any action, would be better than waiting. I went into the guards' room and demanded Andrew's Air Jordans so I could take them to his mother. Earlier in the evening, I had promised Andrew I would let his mother know that he wanted to be buried in them. The guard I spoke with calmly explained that Andrew's effects could only be released to his next of kin and that they would ship the running shoes to Andrew's mother. I knew at that moment that Andrew's mother would not receive the shoes in time for Andrew's funeral.

Shortly after I returned to the main room, eight guards exited the execution chamber holding their hands away from their bodies. They had just removed Andrew's body from the electric chair. They formed a line at the men's rest room and, one by one, washed the touch of his skin off their hands.

Sarah Ottinger
New Orleans, Louisiana
October 1998

THE ANDREW LEE JONES FUND

This fund exists to provide scholarships for individuals studying law in the USA, with a view to practising in the field of capital defence.

The fund is named in memory of Andrew Lee Jones, who died in the electric chair in Louisiana on 22 July 1991. There are some doubts surrounding the evidence brought by the prosecution and mitigating factors that were not considered by the court. Better legal representation at his trial would have ensured that the jury heard all the relevant facts in considering whether to impose the death penalty.

A very large number of the 3,300 individuals on Death Row in the USA owe their plight to inadequate legal representation. Capital defence work is poorly paid, so very few well-qualified lawyers choose to specialize in this field. There is an urgent need for more highly motivated lawyers to prevent further miscarriages of justice.

It is extremely expensive to attend law school in the USA. Fees and living expenses vary between $20,000 and $30,000 per annum over a three-year course of study. US citizens may help with their costs by working part time, but this is generally not permitted for foreign nationals on student visas.

The Andrew Lee Jones Fund therefore seeks to offer scholarships to individuals who have obtained places at an American Bar Association approved law school on a needs basis. Scholarships are also available for students who volunteer to work as interns for short periods as part of their studies.

Patrons: Benjamin Zephaniah, John Mortimer, Ludovic Kennedy, Helena Kennedy QC, Michael Mansfield QC, Clive Stafford Smith, Paul Hamman, Lady Antonia Fraser, Bruce Kent, Ed Asner, A.S. Byatt.

Chairperson: Jane Officer; Secretary: Sophie Garner; Committee: Joanne Cross and Claire Jenkins.

Enquiries and legal matters: Sophie Garner, 199 Strand, London WC2R 1DR.

Donations: Jane Officer, 1 Hemyock Road, Selly Oak, Birmingham B29 4DG. Please make any donations payable to: The Andrew Lee Jones Fund.

ALSO PUBLISHED BY NEW CLARION PRESS

Out of the Night: Writings from Death Row
Edited by Marie Mulvey Roberts with Benjamin Zephaniah
Foreword by the Rt Hon. Michael Foot

A LifeLines Book of the Year

'The contributors to this anthology are writers and poets who live continually under the threat of death. They are introduced to their readers not in the first instance as convicts, who have been found guilty of crimes that carry a capital penalty, but as the collective authorship of *Out of the Night*' (from the Introduction).

This book is the only collection of poems and prose by prisoners on America's Death Row. It lets us hear voices from that terrifying darkness, where 3,300 people face execution. For these authors, their writing is a lifeline and a link to the outside world. They use it to evoke the desolation of imprisonment without hope, and to argue passionately against the inhumanity of capital punishment.

Marie Mulvey Roberts is a writer and senior lecturer in Literary Studies at the University of the West of England, Bristol. She has done a variety of teaching in UK prisons. Benjamin Zephaniah is well known as a poet, performer and political activist.

> '*Out of the Night*, through its first-hand accounts and poetry reflecting unimaginable pain and solitude, paints a vivid picture' *Amnesty International*
>
> 'Earthy, graphic, this is a book that pulls no punches ... easily read but not easily forgotten' *Justice of the Peace and Local Government Law*
>
> 'credit should be given to the compilers for the dedicated intelligence with which they sifted, chose and arranged writings' *Literary Review*

Royalties from the sale of *Out of the Night* are being donated to the Andrew Lee Jones Fund.

256 pages, illustrated
Paperback   £10.95   ISBN 1 873797 09 5
Hardback   £23.50   ISBN 1 873797 10 9

For more information on books published by New Clarion Press:
New Clarion Press, 5 Church Row, Gretton, Cheltenham GL54 5HG
tel./fax 01242 620623